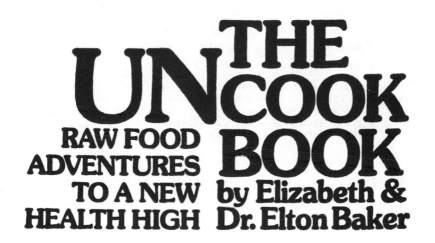

THE UN COOK BOOK

RAW FOOD ADVENTURES TO A NEW HEALTH HIGH

by Elizabeth & Dr. Elton Baker

DRELWOOD COMMUNICATIONS, INC.

P.O. Box 149
Indianola, WA 98342

Although the authors and publisher have exhaustively researched all sources to ensure the accuracy and completeness of the information contained in this book, we assume no responsibility for errors, inaccuracies, omissions or any inconsistency herein. Any slights of people or organizations are unintentional. Readers should use their own judgment, consult a holistic medical expert of their personal physician for specific applications to their individual problems.

Library of Congress Cataloging in Publication Data

Baker, Elizabeth, 1913—
    The uncook book.

    1. Food, Raw.   2. Nutrition.   3. Health.
I. Baker, Elton, 1911-   joint author.   II. Title.
TX392.B29   641.5'637   80-21665
ISBN 0-937766-05-4

ATTENTION HEALTH PROFESSIONALS, SCHOOLS, CORPORATIONS: This book is available at quantity discounts on bulk purchases for patient, educational or promotional use. For information please contact Drelwood Communications, P.O. Box 149 WA 98342

First printing 1981
Second printing 1981
Third printing 1983
Fourth printing 1984
Fifth printing 1989
Sixth printing 1992
Seventh printing 1993

Printed in the United States of America

What People Are Saying

"Readers of natural food cookery and gourmets of all types were delighted to pick up this new reading gem . . . a very easy-to-follow step-by-step approach is laid out by the Bakers as to how to 'withdraw' from the McDonaldized American diet and step into the world of natural cuisine . . . I would give this book the 4 star rating."

Jonathan Collin M.D.
Northwest Academy of Preventive Medicine Newsletter

"Extremely well done and very complete."

C. W. (Bill) Frazier, Jr., President
Frazier Farms Health Food store chain

"An excellent chapter is 'How to Combine Foods for Good Digestion and Moderate Eating.'" In this the old cliche', 'we are what we eat' comes to light."

Bestways Magazine

"I plan on using it for our text book in our nutrition classes. It's the *only* book I've seen so far that I can recommend without reservations."

Sally Rockwell, Nutritionist
The Huxley Institute for Biosocial Research

"The reason why the *UNcook Book* may attract retirees on fixed incomes is money savings. The more of your food you can forage or grow for yourself, the lighter the price of your weekly market basket. Further, the book is going to advise you how to make use of throw-aways such as potato peelings and beet tops."

Jack Smith
Nationally Syndicated Columnist

"*The UNcook Book: Raw Food Adventures to a New Health High* provides information on such problems as how to pack a nourishing workday lunch and what to do when traveling and eating out, and natural recipes for dishes such as Brazil Nut Louie, Raisin Carrot Bread and Salad-of-the-Sun."

Health Food Business Magazine

"This very practical cookbook needs a place on your home shelf . . . a genuine way to vastly improve one's nutrition."

Holistic Medicine
Newsletter of American Holistic Medical Association

Acknowledgments

To Lloyd Silver, M.D. for rescuing us from conventional medical practices and helping us on the natural foods road to health.

To Joseph T. Morgan, M.D., for fasting us to health and teaching us how to discover our allergies.

To Eloise Kalin, M.D. for countinuing guidance in coping with an allery-causing, polluted environment.

To Wm. A. Ellis, D.O., for generously sharing his fund of health information gleaned from forty years of nutritional medical practice.

To Linus Pauling, Ph.D., whose contributions to science and health are closely followed by Elton who as a student met and listened to him lecture.

To Melvin Calvin, Ph.D., under whose wise and inspiring direction Elton participated in research at the University of California.

To Gordon Townsend, D.C., for opening a whole new world of health help through kinesiology.

To Thelma Arthur, M.D., for introducing us to her efficacious method of cancer detection, her help and encouragement in Elizabeth's struggle to health.

Health Institutes

The authors wish to express their gratitude to the Hippocrates Health Institute, 25 Exeter Street, Boston, Massachusetts 02116, and its founder, Dr. Ann Wigmore, and Hippocrates Health Institute of San Diego at 6970 Central Avenue, Lemon Grove, California 92045.

These nonprofit health resorts are dedicated to helping people learn to help themselves through an all-raw diet regime and natural health practices. During our stay at the institutes, we met wonderful people who, like ourselves, were oftentimes made ill by modern conventional medical methods, and were regaining their health by their own efforts and new-found knowledge.

There are many health resorts over the world. Viktoras Kulvinskas in his book *Survival Into The 21st Century* gives a list of these resorts. He also has written a directory, published by Omango D'Press, P.O. Box 64, Woodstock, California 06282.

Foreword

The Bakers' book is an excellent contribution to the field of natural foods. It is a most stimulating and useful guide to implementing nutritional practices which can lead only to better health and improved efficiency of community nutrition policies.

The UNcook Book has successfully accomplished the very difficult task of presenting the topic of natural, uncooked foods in an excitingly palatable and understanding way to people who are used to eating the standard American diet... which is almost opposite of a nutritionally sound and healthful diet.

The recipes are of significant variety to provide an interesting bill of fare. Their ingredients are easily acquired by anyone. This approach makes it possible for the nutritionally-sound recipes to be incorporated by all.

The underlying visionary philosophy of the Bakers' book helps us all to better understand why natural foods (and less processed foods) are more healthful to the individual, beneficial to our community and more efficient in the terms of world food resources. The scope of this message is indeed far-reaching.

I strongly recommend that all people —especially those interested in increased health and well-being—seriously consider incorporating the nutritional philosophies presented in *The UNcook Book.*

Jeffrey S. Bland, Ph.D.

Preface

Whether the word is spelled *holistic* or the modern adaptation, *wholistic*, the intended meaning, according to *Webster's New Collegiate Dictionary*, is the same: *"the functional relation between parts and wholes."* Certainly there is a relation between the "irreducible whole" of the "Body, Mind and Spirit," the three parts of man which the holistic movement is all about.

In the normal individual, Body, Mind and Spirit are so closely related they are an integral part of each other. One cannot function without the other two. Therefore, attention is focused on stressing the nurturing of each without the neglect of any one. For optimal performance, they must be simultaneously treated the way the Creator instructed. Neither Mind nor Spirit can be expected to fulfill without a well-functioning Body. Jesus, surveying the multitude who came to hear Him, first took care of their bodies by healing them. Only after these miracles of healing did He seek to nourish the mind with parables that led to the nourishing of the Spirit. Then He refused to let them be sent away hungry. He performed the miracle of feeding the 5,000 plus women and children with five loaves and two fishes.

In nourishing and caring for our bodies through all-natural foods, cleanliness and excercise, we care for the temple of not only the Mind, but also of the Soul. Then the Mind can seek after truth and knowledge that the Soul may be freed from impediments and ignorance to reach for God.

The reassuring result of seeking to improve any one of the three — Body, Mind, Spirit — is the irreversible start of improving the others. Try fasting a disease-wracked body until it is without sickness, and you will experience such a surge of spiritual uplift, such a clear mind and feeling of well-being that your thoughts will automatically turn to bright and good things. It is then that you fully believe those statements by anthropologists, research nutritionists and physicians, that among those few isolated races of people who still eat a diet of all-natural foods, there are no nervous disorders, no juvenile delinquency, no behavioral distortions, no crimes, no physical or moral decadence.

When Spirit is one with God, the stage is set for maximum function of Body and Mind. When Mind is clear and not distorted by doubts, by physical pain and encumbrance, it is a thing of beauty and serves well. When Body's functions live up to the Creator's plan, Mind and Spirit find no limits of joy and service, fulfillment and love.

The purpose of this book is to help the individual, in taking the responsibility for his or her own health, to achieve an optimally functioning Body through natural, living foods. In so doing, one will quite naturally find oneself nourishing Mind and Spirit, thus traveling the road to holistic health. There can be no other way...for it is God's way.

Table of Contents

List of
Charts and Tables

Introduction

A wonderful new movement has started in America. It promises to be one of the greatest to sweep the country since pioneer days drew settlers west to develop the wilderness. We are speaking of the movement among adults to take *responsibility* for their own health —or their recovery from disease through proper nutrition.

With the highest incidence of disease of any nation in the world, Americans need this bright ray of hope. Many factors have contributed to the present eroding state of health —or lack of it. We are paying the price of industrial development and sophistication with a lagging awareness and provision for protecting the environment from pollution. Commercially-grown, sprayed and dusted crops, air pollution, bad water, highly processed foods with drastic loss of nutritional content and the overproduction and misuse of drugs have all contributed to health degeneration.

But there is yet another factor, all too often overlooked. Adults of this century have relinquished their right to care for their own health and dumped the responsibility onto their doctors. The burden, however, is impossible for medical professionals to bear. Not only are they untrained in finding the basic cause of disease or to determine a rejuvenating nutritional regimen, but they also tend to overprescribe surgery and drugs.

Drugs may suppress or stimulate and so alleviate symptoms...and, may destroy virus and bacteria. Surgery may remove the diseased results of a wrongly-treated body. Yet, neither gets to the cause of the disease. If nothing is done to remove the cause, the conventionally-treated patient is vulnerable to a recurrence of the same disease —plus others —as a result of the toxins and shock from drug treatment and/or surgery. The cause is usually not only nutritional, but how well or poorly the body digests and absorbs what it takes in.

There is a way to treat the cause. That way is open to all adults who accept the responsibility for their own health. We only need to embrace the universally accepted idea that given the essential repair nutrients, the body heals itself. This fact frees us from needing to waste time learning about disease, diagnoses, physiology, or biochemistry. We only have to learn what and how to eat and drink to provide our bodies with all the essential maintenance and repair materials to keep or restore health. It doesn't matter whether we have arthritis, diseased kidneys, cancer, other degenerative diseases...or simply a red, bulbous nose. They will all disappear if the body is given an optimal diet and some time to detoxify and heal itself as nature intended.

What are we waiting for? Let us welcome the challenge of this exciting new adventure — a bold entry into a bright future for the Mind, the Spirit and the Body God gave us "to keep holy".

Elizabeth and Dr. Elton Baker

Why An All-Raw Diet

*"The doctor of the future will give no medi-
cine, but will interest his patient in the care of
the human frame, in diet and in the cause and
prevention of disease."*

Thomas A. Edison

The question most frequently asked of us today is, "Why vegetarianism?" That question invariably leads to a host of others. One of the askers of those questions was a scientist friend who recently visited us. He was shocked to learn that "sensible people" like the Bakers had chosen, as he put it, "to waste away on a vegetarian diet."

Because his questions represented a composite of those asked by our lecture audiences, students and friends, we recorded it. We will call our friend the **Interviewer**. In our work of lecturing and teaching together, we may not notice where one leaves off and the other begins in a discussion-answer session. Therefore, we identify our conversations as simply —**Bakers.** What follows is that interview.

Interviewer: When did you become vegetarians and why?
Bakers: Eight years ago "terminal" illness forced us, as a last resort, to turn to nutrition. All the conventional medical routes had been exhausted. At the end of the road, we began to read all we could find on nutrition against disease and nutrition for health. First off, we eliminated table sugar and white flour. All processed foods soon followed, and organic foods were introduced into our diet. Our health began to improve dramatically. Elton overcame hypertension, asthma and glaucoma and Elizabeth overcame arthritis, bursitis, constipation, headaches, hypoglycemia, stiff joints and the like, as well as the "terminal" illness of Addison's disease. Most of her problems steadily disappeared. One persisted. Later we learned it was cancer of the colon.

We both started to eat all-raw foods. It was only three years ago. Now the cancer of the colon is almost gone. Skin cancers are all gone.

Interviewer: That's remarkable. And you both look great. But to say the least, an all-raw diet seems pretty drastic.

Bakers: It was to us. It is for most conventional eaters. To change to an all-raw diet means giving up a lot of foods they've been accustomed to.

Interviewer: What do you mean by a conventional eater?

Bakers: The meat–potatoes–gravy–small salad–canned green beans - apple pie and coffee eater who has bacon, eggs, white toast, orange drink and coffee for breakfast and a salami sandwich, carrot sticks, oatmeal cookie and milk or coffee for lunch with cokes and/or beer between meals.

Interviewer: That's a pretty well-balanced diet, isn't it?

Bakers: By conventional standards.

Interviewer: What's wrong with a conventional diet?

Bakers: A conventional diet is woefully lacking in nutrition. The much touted "balanced diet" almost always disregards the actual nutritional content of the products ending up on the family dinner table. So many are processed and as such, nutritionally depleted.

Interviewer: Would you explain why an all-raw diet is desirable? Beneficial?

Bakers: In the beginning, God told man what to eat. "Behold, I have given you every plant yielding seed which is upon the face of all the earth, and every tree with seed in its fruit; you shall have them for food." Genesis 1:29. Much later God's prophet said, "— and the fruit thereof shall be for meat and the leaves thereof for medicine." Ezekiel 47:12. Fruits, vegetables (herbs), seeds, nuts and grains in the raw state have all the nutrients necessary to maintain optimal health and longevity. Nowhere in the Bible does God tell man to cook these foods. Man probably stumbled onto the act of "killing" his food with fire, quite by accident.

Cooking foods destroys from 30% to 85% of the nutrition. All of this destroyed, deficient, altered food must be disposed of by the body God created to ingest the living foods that nature produces for it. Cooked and chemicalized foods are foreign to the body. Foreign substances in the body are toxic to it because it is not made to digest and utilize them. It is forced to cope with them as best it can.

Interviewer: You've answered the question of why an all-raw diet is more beneficial. But I'm not convinced it is desirable.

Bakers: As a matter of fact, it sounds quite undesirable to most of us who've been brought up on a conventional diet. From babyhood to the grave, we as a nation are accustomed to mostly cooked foods. Fortunately, despite increased advertising of processed foods, the general public is becoming more natural-food and raw-food conscious. More and more restaurants are featuring a salad bar, and sprouts are at least familiar in name and sight to many people.

But to get back to the desirability of eating uncooked foods.

• Fresh, raw foods contain all the nutrients necessary for good health, growth, maintenance and repair.

• Raw foods are easily digested (24 to 36 hours compared to 48 to 100 hours for cooked foods).

• Raw foods provide more energy for the body. Much less energy is wasted digesting toxins which the body must struggle to eliminate.

• Raw foods cost less — kitchen-grown sprouts from seeds and grains, fresh vegetables and fruits from your deck pots or garden. No costly condiments and seasonings to buy. No waste, shrinkage or loss as with cooked foods.

• Raw foods are easier to prepare.

• Raw foods are much easier to clean up after — no greasy skillets, pots, pans, dishes, stoves, sinks, walls, ceilings.

• Raw foods help the body to achieve a normal weight. Obesity disappears steadily, painlessly, effortlessly.

• Raw foods restore the natural *appestat* (appetite control) — it is difficult to overeat on a raw-food diet.

• Raw foods do not cause or support degenerative diseases.

• Raw foods help a person feel better, have more energy, rest better and spend less time sleeping.

• Raw foods eliminate body odor and halitosis.

• Raw foods clear up menstruation and menopausal problems.

• On raw foods, the mind — memory, power of concentration, ability to reason — will be clearer.

• On raw foods, a person is not troubled with incontinence.

• Raw foods help a person be calm and emotionally stable.

• On a raw-food diet, there are not the swings from "high" to "low" one experiences on a conventional diet of stimulants (sugar, coffee, tea, coke, small amounts of alcohol) and depressants (heavy rich foods, overeating, too much alcohol, over-the-counter drugs).

• On a raw food regimen, one feels closer to God because of eating the way He wanted us to eat and feeling (physically and mentally) the way He intended us to feel.

Interviewer: You make a strong case. Raw foods are fine. They may be according to nature. But don't you think nature is a bit overrated? After all, science is adding a tremendous number of things to mankind's comfort, benefit and well-being.

Bakers: But it's also contributing greatly to his downfall. On grocery shelves there sit more than 5,000 items processed from whole natural foods into empty edibles that are indigestible because of heat and toxic chemicals. It has helped earn for our country the dubious distinction of having the most unhealthy population in the world. Less than 1% of the people are truly, completely healthy.

Some 65% of American adults and 20% of children under 17 now live with chronic disease and medication. Most of the others are self-treated with aspirin, tranquilizers, alkalizers, laxatives, cold and flu remedies, alcohol and so on. A comparative few are vegetarian, eating a simple diet and enjoying physical and mental health.

Interviewer: I've heard that vegetarians live longer than meat-eaters. Is this true?

Bakers: Yes. And they have far fewer degenerative diseases.

Interviewer: But they do have some.

Bakers: With the pollution of air and water, and pollution entering the skin from scented soaps and cosmetics, plastics and polyester clothing, both of which *gas-off* their toxins continuously — no one today can escape a certain amount of harm from pollution. The least we can do is eliminate artificial and overcooked foods.

Interviewer: You make the outlook seem hopeless.

Bakers: Quite the contrary. There's something everyone can do. Eat to live.

Interviewer: Isn't that what most everyone does?

Bakers: That is their intention. But they do not eat to live *well*. They eat polluted food. It is impossible to live well (by that we mean live with good health), while eating a diet of overcooked, mainly processed, inorganically-grown food. There are too many substances in them that are completely foreign to the body. And anything that is foreign to the body becomes a toxin. Something that the eliminative organs have to throw off. The lungs, skin, kidneys and bowels are our eliminative organs. Toxins put a strain on them, especially since these organs are all suffering deficiencies from processed, overcooked and chemicalized non-foods. Not only are processed foods woefully deficient in nutriments, they are so addictive that most people overeat much of the time. The use of sugar and artificial flavors have made foods heavenly in the mouth and hellish in the system. Many physicians, nutritionists and hygienists believe that overeating is our biggest health problem.

Interviewer: I've read that about half the population in America today is overweight.

Bakers: Forgive us for repeating a cliche, but it is so appropos:

America is overfed and undernourished.

Overeating causes emotional and mental problems, too. No wonder the Bible lists gluttony as one of the sins (Proverbs). It's so harmful to our body and to our mind. The raw food scientist and author Kulvinskas said, "When one eats a heavy meal his energy goes from his head to his stomach." All too often physical sluggishness translates to mental sluggishness.

One of the rewards of eating an all-natural, mainly raw diet is a clearer head, a more positive outlook, increased ability to cope with the stresses and frustrations of modern living. It provides us the foundation for greater spiritual awareness.

Interviewer: Isn't it prohibitively expensive for a lot of people to eat a raw diet? One look at the price of fresh vegetables and fruits scares most of us away. We have to settle for pizza. Frozen orange juice. Canned corn.

Bakers: The raw-food dieter eats well on from 25% to 80% less money than does the conventional eater. And in so doing sustains better health, a slimmer figure, a more tranquil emotional status.

Interviewer: I have pretty good health. I just live with a few little things like dandruff, some varicose veins from being on my feet too much in the lab, a touch of high blood pressure. No more than most of us live with. But I'd surely like to cut down on my grocery bill. I'd like you to explain how to do that...the impossible.

Bakers: All right. First I'd like to assure you, you don't have to live with the ills...or the bills. Let me give you a few comparisons on costs. One big raw apple costs about 20¢. It has more nutrition than three canned or cooked apples at 50¢. One carrot at 8¢ has more nutrition than three cooked ones, costing 24¢. For a person even to approach the nourishment of one raw apple or one raw carrot, he has to eat at least three cooked ones. Translated to a full meal, that means overeating and overspending without counting the cost of the gas or electricity for cooking or the time and labor involved in preparation.

Interviewer: But what about protein? Meat? That's the most expensive part of a meal.

Bakers: It may be the most expensive item of a conventional meal. It's costly to buy, costly to cook, costly in the waste of nutrients in the heat, time-consuming in the preparation and serving, and all too often costly in the toll it takes on one's health.

Interviewer: Why is it necessarily costly to health? I've always been told and I've also read that we have to eat meat to obtain protein for body maintenance and repair.

Bakers: Meat — all animal proteins — is more difficult to digest. Many people do not have a digestive system adequate to digest meat and animal products well. They are among those especially susceptible to cancer. The enzymes in cooked meat have been largely destroyed by heat. It's up to the body to produce (if it's still capable) enough enzymes to digest it. Partly because of the lack of enzymes and partly because of slow-digesting fat, the intestines need from 60 to 100 hours to digest animal protein. In this slowed-down process, the food becomes putrefactive with bad bacteria. The (bad) bacteria in turn destroy the (good) intestinal flora that synthesizes B vitamins. Bad bacteria are self-perpetuating and the indirect cause of much degenerative disease.

Sufficient and complete protein is available in the vegetarian diet. There's all sorts of nuts, grains, seeds and sprouts, especially legumes. Sprouts are the most delicious, inexpensive and nutritious of the protein foods. Take alfalfa sprouts... it's a complete protein legume and one of the best sources, not only for protein but for taste, vitamins, minerals and enzymes. A pound of alfalfa seeds at the co-op costs $2.00 ($1.45 at a grower's farm, $2.65 at health food stores). It takes two ounces (three tablespoons) of seeds to make a pound of sprouts costing at most 45¢, at the least 23¢. In supermarkets, sprouts cost on an average of $1.55 a pound. You can see how little this super food costs when you grow your own in a jar any time of the year, in any climate. In addition, sprouting converts the protein to amino acids which means that sprouts are essentially predigested.

Interviewer: To go suddenly from meats, poultry and fish to alfalfa is revolutionary. Is that what you advise people to do?

Bakers: No. There isn't one in 1,000, probably, that would or could do it. We advocate — suggest — that people first eliminate sugar and white flour, the empty calorie foods from their diet. After adjusting to that, they should start eliminating all processed foods. Just launching out on an all-natural food diet, even mostly cooked, will take discipline and planning. However, if fresh sprouts are added to *all* cooked foods, and we do mean all — mashed or baked potatoes, salads, gravies, sandwiches, casseroles, vegetable dishes, fruit sauces and juice beverages — the transition from conventional foods to all-raw foods will be much easier. And the sprouts help one to start feeling better right away.

Interviewer: How long does it take to go from a transitional diet to an all-raw one?

Bakers: That depends on the person or family. A year is not unrealistic. Elton took longer, Elizabeth much less —only a few days because of the terminal illness. Motivation is the determining factor. We feel that someone in a transitional period should try very hard not to go back to the old way of eating, but certainly should not feel guilty or discouraged at going on a binge or backsliding once in a while. Many people on a conventional diet are food addicts and most Americans are sugar addicts. Cravings can be intense. But indulgences should get farther and farther apart as progress is made in the transition. Even though a person has to eat out frequently, there are foods he can find. (See Chapter XI.)

Interviewer: I'd like to go back to something you mentioned earlier...cooked foods and fats digesting more slowly.

Bakers: Yes. Dr. Pottenger of Monrovia, California, did extensive experimentation on animals. When he fed them cooked foods, their mucous membranes began to thicken and run, and they contracted allergy symptoms and respiratory infections. Later he discovered the same thing happened to his patients. And people with sick membranes are sick all over —bad digestion, sluggish glands, arthritic joints, a red nose. Deficiencies affect the whole body. It's just that a person is aware of one area of the body more than another.

Interviewer: I never really thought about it. But since all the cells in the system need nutrients of all kinds, it stands to reason that deficiencies could show up in any part of it.

Bakers: Yes, the weakest part, the most misused part. The body needs maximum nutrition for maintenance and repair.

Interviewer: Aren't proteins utilized for maintenance and repair? That still means meat, poultry, fish, eggs, milk.

Bakers: Of course, those are all high sources of protein. But up to 85% of the nutrition in meat can be destroyed by cooking. Some vegetarian nutritionists and physicians say there are a few people who are animal food metabolizers (we have not knowingly encountered any). These people cannot maintain good health on a vegetarian diet, scientists maintain. These scientists warn, however, that all possible fat should be removed before cooking meat.

Interviewer: It's pretty much accepted that animal fats should be avoided and polyunsaturated fats used instead.

Bakers: We advocate avoiding all fats except those that occur naturally in seeds, nuts and avocado. Natural oil in the diet is an essential nutrient. Not heat-treated oils. Heat ruins them. It's appalling what heated fats do to the human body.

Interviewer: But cold-pressed oils are recommended, aren't they?

Bakers: Not any more. A lot of research has been done recently on so-called cold-pressed oils. But there is no such thing as cold-pressed oil. It's simply a word applied to the least heat-treated process of extracting oil. The oil of seeds, grains or nuts is pressed out by large rollers, but the pressure heats the oil so hot when it comes out it would burn your hand.

Not only is the oil unavoidably heated, the seeds, grains and nuts that are used are the culls — the inferior, molded, diseased, grade of the crops. Chemical treatment (solvents) take out the natural odor, the color and the sediment to give a clear, colorless, tasteless oil, and preservatives are added to allow for an indefinite shelf-life. You don't even have to refrigerate such oil. Animals and insects will not voluntarily eat it, and humans shouldn't. We're amazed that people are as healthy as they are eating oils and other processed foods with all the chemicals (poisons) in them.

Interviewer: We've been told for a long time that they lower blood cholesterol.

Bakers: They will do just that. Polyunsaturated oil makes the cholesterol fine-particled so that it readily goes into the veins and arteries. But there it sticks. By so doing it causes more hardening of the arteries than saturated animal fats.

Interviewer: That's amazing. For years we've all been advised to eat polyunsaturated oil.

Bakers: That's true. We consumed our share, too. Then we began to read some of the findings of research of the last few years. We were shocked to think of all the harm we had done by giving people erroneous advice. One of the best articles written for the non-professional is a chapter on the oils and the chemical changes made in them by commercial processors, in the book *Food for Naught,* by Dr. Ross Hall. As another doctor said, "If man made it, don't eat it."

Interviewer: It's difficult to realize oils do great harm.

Bakers: To oversimplify: Sugars and cooked fats tend to cause the red blood cells to adhere to each other. For instance, after a person eats a meal with the present-day level of fats, oils, refined carbohydrates, sugars and sugar-like foods, the red blood cells stick together. When these clumps reach the capillary beds, the place where the blood of the arteries turns and goes into the veins, they clog the circulation. There's a stagnation and a leakage of fluids into tissues all over the body, including the brain. It's a great cause of water retention (edema). Many have experienced water-logging headaches after eating a meal high in fats, oils, sugars and/or sweets.

Interviewer: What fats should one avoid?

Bakers: Canned fish in oil and all processed meats that contain considerable fats and chemicals. Ham, bacon, sausage, lunch meats, wieners, over-the-counter hamburger. If meat, poultry or fish is eaten, all the fat possible should be removed. You'll still have 10% to 15% fat laced through it. Most of the toxins fed to the animal go into its fat. You're getting a certain amount even after cutting off all the fat you can. And don't charcoal broil. The fumes from the briquettes are poisonous and the fats are usually overcooked — charred. Such meats are known to be carcinogenic (cancer-producing).

Other no-no's are all fried foods, margarine, mayonnaise and most salad dressings. Only a very little cold-pressed oil (the least bad of the lot) with a little lemon juice or vinegar.

One should gradually phase out oil as a dressing and cultivate the exquisite natural tastes of the vegetables in the salad. We make dressings of avocados or seed and nut meats or raw tofu blended with sprout soak water or fermec (see Chapter IX). These natural foods contain all the fresh oils essential for health.

Interviewer: What about butter?

Bakers: Pure butter is a natural food nutrient. However, one should eat no more than a small pat at a meal and then only if the intestines can take care of it.

Interviewer: Apparently a low-fat diet is what keeps vegetarians thin. Why is this so?

Bakers: Certainly it's a contributing factor. It's almost impossible to gain weight if you eat very little fat. Let's look at three basic nutrition essentials — protein, carbohydrates and fat. A gram of protein has four calories. A gram of carbohydrate has four calories. A gram of fat has nine calories. On a conventional diet, one gets a lot of fat. The average person ingests 30 grams of fat a day. That person needs only 5 to 15.

Interviewer: I'm beginning to understand why protein is stressed in so many reducing diets.

Bakers: Sometimes they are overstressed and that's not good, especially for reducing. The body utilizes protein only for maintenance and repair. Any protein left over is converted to calories. If not burned by exercise and physical activity, it is stored in the body as fat. The average American eater of animal products (meats, poultry, dairy foods, eggs, seafoods) gets 60 to 120 grams of protein a day. Biochemists have found that somewhere between 25 and 45 grams of complete protein, depending on the size and metabolism of the adult, are needed to maintain good health.

Interviewer: Isn't it very difficult to get enough protein on a vegetarian diet?

Bakers: It simply takes a little studying and planning like any other program does.

For example, here's a raw food regimen for a medium-sized adult for a day with an adequate amount of digestible complete protein:

Breakfast — One whole, thinly peeled cantaloupe with seeds made into a milk in the blender. Seven grams of protein.

Lunch — Two slices sprouted rye Essene bread with walnuts, Green pea soup. Relish dish of carrots and cauliflower. Twelve grams protein.

Supper — Very large green salad of sprouts (mung bean, alfalfa, buckwheat lettuce), parsley, celery, carrots, etc. with avocado-lemon dressing, sprouted buckwheat crackers and homemade soy cheese. Seventeen grams protein.

Total protein grams for a day — 36 grams

Interviewer: Since eating the pea soup and Essene nut bread we had for lunch, I'm beginning to feel differently about a vegetarian diet. But without eating meat, where does a vegetarian get Vitamin B_{12}, the anti-pernicious anemia factor?

Bakers: We're glad you asked that question. Recently, research information on Vitamin B_{12} was reported at a symposium. It was reported that a certain bacteria in the intestine supplies man's needs. This applies to animals also, for that matter. With healthy intestines and sufficient cobalt from such foods as alfalfa, plankton and green leafy vegetables, bacteria will produce vitamin B_{12}.

Interviewer: Then if this certain bacteria provides Vitamin B_{12}, why is there considerable pernicious anemia?

Bakers: Today it's difficult to find a truly healthy intestinal tract among conventional eaters of processed foods. Because of too much sugar, too many protein foods, overeating, wrong and complex food combinations, polluted air, lack of enzymes, plant and insect sprays, and chemically treated water, the intestinal walls are made impermeable to all vitamins by slimy mucus. The person with such intestines naturally suffers a vitamin deficiency. But such a person can correct the condition by avoiding sugar, refined starch (white flour, white rice) and animal proteins. He or she should eat lots of green vegetables, especially the leafy green ones and mostly raw, never eating when not hungry, and never overeating. Meals should be very simple and foods in the right combination.

Interviewer: I notice you stress the eating of leafy green vegetables. Is that for everybody?

Bakers: We'd like to recommend them to everybody. Leafy green vegetables are cleansers of the digestive system. They have bulk, an abundance of vitamins, minerals and chlorophyll (nature's healer). Watch a cat or dog. What's the first thing it eats — if available — when first let out early in the morning? Grass. What's the first thing a sick animal eats after fasting itself through the illness? Grass.

Interviewer: Yes, I've seen animals eat grass. Is it because of the healing chlorophyll?

Bakers: That's surely part of the reason. No doubt it has all the health-giving enzymes, minerals (like potassium, magnesium, calcium, etc.) and vitamins. Plenty of Vitamin A is needed to clear up sick mucous membranes (mouth, sinuses, ears, eyes, digestive tract). Grass contains an abundance of this vitamin. "—And their eyes did fail because there was no grass." Jeremiah 14:5, 6.

Interviewer: I notice you stress grass and chlorophyll, and you grow wheat grass. That seems to be catching on with a lot of people, for whatever reason.

Bakers: Yes. It's a very good sign. A sign that people are taking the responsibility for getting and staying well. Wheat grass is a complete food containing all the known essential nutrients. Many experiments have been made the last few years on the nutrition in grasses, with wheat at the head of the list.

Some 25 years ago, Dr. Ann Wigmore started experimenting with feeding animals the grasses and found that wheat grass was the one instinctively preferred by them. She also had, as a child, much experience with the effectiveness of grass for health and healing. As a result, she established the highly respected Hippocrates Health Institute in Boston. Hundreds of people from all over the world have through the years attended the institute to learn to grow wheat grass and sprouts and go on an all-raw diet. The institute encourages city dwellers to take two ounces of wheat grass juice a day to protect themselves from air pollution, and people struggling to overcome degenerative disease to take two ounces three times a day. Over a period of time — weeks or months — there's a noticeable difference in health and energy.

Interviewer: I always associate grass with animals, not people.
Bakers: All of us do. But the ancients also associated it with people. "All flesh is grass." I Peter 1:24.

Elizabeth grew up on a midwestern wheat farm where cattle and horses were turned onto wheat grass pasture for the winter. The animals' flesh grew firm, their coats thick and shiny. She can never remember having a sick animal. (The nearest veterinarian was 120 miles away.) The cows' milk production increased phenomenally, the butterfat content went up with an increase of all vitamins, especially Vitamins A and C. Humans benefit as much as cattle and horses from wheat grass. It's a great way to get the vitamins one needs at only pennies a day.

Interviewer: You've given me a lot to think about. I thank you for answering my questions.

How To Start Your Health-Improving Diet

"If anyone consults a doctor after the age of 30, he is a fool, since by that time everyone should know how to regulate his life properly."
Tiberius, A.D. 30

The Transitional Program

You've read and heard of the diet of the future—the unfired (uncooked) regimen that insures good health and remission from bad health. You're convinced you should try it, but you don't know how or where to start.

Don't panic!

Just read on.

Step 1. Go to your cupboards, find all sugar and white flour and rid your kitchen of it.

For a week or so prepare your family's meals in your customary way, but without sugar and white flour. This means, for instance, making pancakes out of buckwheat; cakes, cookies, pizza, pie crust and bread out of whole wheat flour; using 1/3 as much honey for sweetener as sugar the recipes call for. Start making breads, muffins and pancakes without any sweetener.

Even this first short easy step will make you so aware of the vast quantities of sugar and white flour baking goods lurking in your marketplace that you'll begin to avoid them.

Step 2. After a week or two, or even three (each household sets its own pace), start eliminating the processed foods from your shelves. Begin with things like prepared gelatins that are artificially flavored, artificially colored and sugar-packed. Carry on with tinned foods and such processed meats as ham, bacon, sausage, lunch meats. Then continue with the disposal of margarine, clear oils,

25

shortenings (good bread can be made without any kind of fat) bottled condiments (except pure, aged soy sauce), packaged cookies, chips and white flour crackers, prepared cereals (except natural granola) and all pastas. Don't forget to eliminate the sodas, cokes and juice drinks.

Step 3. This is the exciting step. The adventurous one. Your step into the future. It takes you to the all-natural foods. Read the list of *Foods to Buy* in Chapter III and decide which ones to start with. You can buy them in the supermarket, local grocery store, farmers market, summer market or roadstand. Besides fresh vegetables and fruits, you'll find nuts and, hopefully, raw peanuts, unsweetened grated coconut, whole fresh coconut, and dry beans, peas, garbanzos and lentils. The last two you can sprout. Get sprouting seeds in health and natural food stores, co-ops or supply catalogs. (See the Appendix for mail order food sources.)

Step 4. Prepare these foods in your customary way. Be very careful not to overcook anything. The longer and hotter the cooking time, the more the nutrients are destroyed and the greater is the chemical change. Do not pour vegetable cooking water — called pot liquor — down the drain. Drink it, serve as a vegetable consommé or use in soups. Fruits make an excellent breakfast, between meal snacks, desserts, even whole meals.

Step 5. At first, start sprouting alfalfa, mung beans and lentils. Gradually introduce other seeds to your indoor sprouting "garden" as you become accustomed to your new routine. (See Chapter VIII for sprouting directions.) Then include sprouts in *all* cooked dishes when they have cooled down enough for you to hold your hand on the bottom of the pan or dish. This will preserve the enzymes in the sprouts and provide the best eating temperature for your health. Eating and drinking hot foods is bad for the mouth (saliva glands), throat and stomach. Add sprouts to sandwiches, vegetables, potato salad, tossed salads, tacos, enchiladas and pizza. Alfalfa and mung bean sprouts are especially good in fruit salads or sprinkled over a fresh fruit plate.

Step 6. You are now over the most time-consuming part of your transition from conventional food fadism to the back-to-nature diet of the future…the diet that will set you free of illness/free of most food pollution/free from kitchen cooking and cleanup drudgery /free of tight food budget worries.

One by one, you'll eliminate cooked foods as your taste changes, as you feel better, as your weight begins to normalize. The natural changes are pleasantly slower changes. As you go along, they work little miracles in your life, like awakening each morning bright-eyed, rested, anticipating—rather than dreading—the day ahead of you. Small annoyances you lived with and accepted as your lot in life will disappear—a facial twitch, dandruff, athlete's foot, the pain of arthritis, tachycardia, migraine headache and so on. And as live foods replace the cooked ones, your energy will increase.

To help you get started, here are typical conventional menus of an American family, some suggested ones for starting your transitional diet and some all-raw ones.

Conventional Menus

Hearty Breakfast
Orange juice
Bacon and eggs, fried
White flour pancakes with margarine and syrup
Coffee

Light Breakfast
Fruit juice
White toast, sweet roll or doughnut
Coffee

Lunch
Meat (salami-cheese) sandwich
Pickle
Two oatmeal cookies
Coke

All-Natural Transitional Menus

Hearty Breakfast
Whole, undyed orange
Soft-boiled or soft-scrambled (no oil) eggs, sprinkled with raw sunflower seeds
All-buckwheat pancakes with butter, honey or pure maple syrup
Herb tea or "Fig Coffee"

Light Breakfast
Fresh fruit
Whole grain toast, butter
Herb tea

Lunch
Romaine leaf sandwich filled with mashed avocado and water-packed tuna
Carrot sticks (or any root vegetable)
Thermos of iced mint tea

Dinner	Dinner
Barbequed beef cubes in sauce	Slow-baked beef cubes au jus
White rice	Brown rice
Buttered peas	Fresh or frozen peas warmed to 104° and buttered (slightly)
Iceberg lettuce salad with French dressing	Spinach, celery and tomato salad with oil, vinegar and favorite seasoning
Hot white rolls with margarine	
Berry pie	Herb tea and honey (optional)
Black tea, mints	

You will notice that the above menus do not follow food combining instructions as given in Chapter V. That will come later. Do not feel guilty if you aren't following those instructions to the letter at the beginning of your change from conventional fare to nutrition of the future. Too drastic and immediate a change can make one feel bewildered, overwhelmed and insecure. And a sudden change is sometimes too taxing for the human organism and may cause upset stomach, indigestion, headache, etc., because of the body cleansing brought about by eating green vegetables. Let yourself stay on the transitional diet until your body adjusts to it and you truly are enjoying the food. It is infinitely better than a conventional regimen. Some people find such improvement in health on the transitional phase they never get to the all-raw part of the program. Yet that is the main goal, the goal that will insure us freedom from degenerative disease.

Menus for the All-Raw Diet of Living Foods
(Diet of the Future)

Breakfast	Lunch	Dinner	Supper
2 medium apples, unpeeled	Salad of green sprouts with avocado	Corn soup	Apple
1 - 2″ x 3″ slice of soy or seed cheese	Tomato dressing	Buckwheat cracker	Berries, fresh frozen or pureed, served over it
	2 slices Essene bread	Slices of raw potato, jicama or Jerusalem artichoke	Sprouted sunflower seeds
	6-10 nuts, soaked a few hours	Seed cheese	

The all-raw menus may appear skimpy to the person considering change from a conventional diet. However, as progress is made, you will notice that as the quality of the food goes up, the quantity eaten goes down. With the *appestat* functioning again, one is not so tempted to overeat. Since the body will utilize the complete nutrition in all-raw foods far more efficiently than in devitalized cooked foods, it will require less quantity. Not only will health go up, food costs will come down.

The recipes that follow can all be eaten on a transitional diet. Only a few foods will be excluded from your all-natural, all-raw regimen. By the time you are ready for the optimal, nutritional, money-saving way of eating, you will not miss the absence of the following foods:

Cold pressed oils

Steamed vegetables

Wrong food combinations

Seasonings except kelp and other sea plants which are very
important foods to continue using

Spices and condiments

Garlic, onions and all members of the lily family. (See
Appendix.)

Butter and cream

With food prices and inflation what they are today, everyone is looking for ways to save money. This book tells you how, step by step, and gives you good health and freedom from degenerative disease in the process.

Not only is money saved on foods, it is saved on trips and time for shipping, on fuel (gas, electricity, oil, wood, coal) because of no heat required for preparation, on cleaning, redecorating. But you may save the most on health and sickness care. Dr. Ann Wigmore says, *"Be Your Own Doctor."* We say, "Exert your right to take the responsibility for your own health."

The Fruitarian Diet — The Ultimate Fare

In all of creation, man's physiology most closely resembles the frugivorous gorilla whose life is free of degenerative disease. The fruitarian way of life — fruits and their seeds — is the ultimate for man, just as God instructed in the beginning. A few people have achieved this goal already. Many see that when civilization returns to God's goal for man, it will have gone full cycle and God's plan will have been accomplished.

What Foods To Buy
And Where To Buy Them

"That our granaries may be full, affording all manner of store;"

Psalms 144:13

You've made the decision to change from conventional foods to natural ones. Suddenly it hits you. No more buying of all those processed and prepared edibles. "But what else is there to buy?" you ask yourself. "How shall we survive? Can we cope with this new Spartan way of life?"

Rest assured. You will have more variety than ever to eat. There are many things —and less expensive— in store for you. A whole new life lies ahead, not just a diet. You won't be plunged into it cold. You'll go step by comfortable step.

Remember that you are going into your new adventure in living one step at a time. Your first step is eliminating table sugar and white flour. The inner voice of your former self says, "Oh, but a little sugar and white flour once in awhile won't hurt any of us." Then the voice of your other self, the self that made the decision, counters, "Any bite of food that is not health-giving is health-destroying."

With sweet fruits replacing sugary desserts and snacks, with whole grain flours serving you well for breads, pancakes, thickening, etc., you carry on for a little while —several days or a few weeks. And while you are discovering how easy, how rewarding it is to live without sugar, white flour and their products, you're already thinking brown rice instead of pastas, dates instead of after dinner TV candies. You are steaming (for only three to eight minutes) instead of boiling your vegetables, and poaching or slightly broiling or baking in low heat your fish, chicken and meats. Already you are enjoying not having to clean so much grease from dishes, pots, pans, sink, stove, walls and ceilings.

You have even given up the popular stir-fry method of preparing vegetables. While less harmful than fast-pan frying or deep-fat frying with their intense heat, it nevertheless destroys much of the nutrition in vegetables (including Vitamin E) by coating them with indigestible heated oil and makes them a hazard to your digestive system.

The alphabetical lists of foods that follow are also alphabetically arranged in groups for clarity and quick, easy reference. At first you will probably want to buy only a fraction of the things listed, but it will be fun to locate and see them when you do your initial natural food shopping.

Cereal Grains

Barley	Millet	Rice	Triticale
Buckwheat*	Oats	Rye	Wheat
Corn			

*While serving as a cereal grain, buckwheat is actually a vegetable.

Grasses for Juicing and Dehydrating
(See Cereal Grains)

Legumes

Alfalfa	(Beans, cont.)	Black-eyed peas	Garbanzos
Beans	Lima	(cowpeas)	(chickpeas)
Adzuki	Mung	Clover	Lentils
Black	Navy	Dahl	Peanuts
Haba (broad)	Pinto		Soybean
	Red Kidney		Cashew

Vegetables

Artichoke	Chive*	Bibb, Boston	Potato
Asparagus	Corn	Iceberg	Pumpkin
Beans, green	Comfrey	(head)*	Radish
Lima	Cucumber	Leaf	Rutabaga
Navy	Dandelion	Romaine	Soybean,
Red Kidney	Eggplant	Mushrooms	Immature
etc.	Endive	Mustard Greens	Spinach
Beets	Garlic*	Okra	Squash
Broccoli	Kale	Onions*	Summer
Brussel Sprouts	Kohlrabi	Parsley	Winter
Cabbage	Lambsquarter	Parsnips	Sweet Potato
Carrots	Leeks*	Peas	Tomato
Cauliflower	Lentils	Peppers	Turnip
Celery	Lettuce	Sweet Green	Water
Chard		Sweet Red	Chestnut
			Watercress

Recommended only on transitional regimen

Fruits

Apple	Date	Loquat	Plum
Apricot	Elderberry	Mandarin	Prune
Avocado	Gooseberry	Orange	Pumpkin
Banana	Grapefruit	Mango	Raisin
Blackberry	Grape — all	Muskmelon	Raspberry
Blueberry	kinds	Nectarine	Rhubarb
Boysenberry	Guava	Olive	Strawberry
Cantaloupe	Honeydew	Orange	Tangerine
Cranberry	Kumquat	Pear	Watermelon
Current	Lemon	Persimmon	Zapote
	Lime	Pineapple	

Nuts

Almond	Filbert	Pecan	Walnut, black
Brazil Nut	(Hazelnut)	Pinon	Walnut, English
Cashew	Macadamia	Pistachio	
(legume)	Peanut (legume)		

Oils

Buy only those with "no preservatives, no chemicals, no solvents" on the label

Almond*	Peanut*	Safflower*	Soy*
Olive†	Pumpkin Seed*	Sesame*	Sunflower*

* *Allowed on transitional diet*
† *Recommended: cold pressed and containing its green chlorophyll*

Protein, Natural Oil Seeds

"Seeds and nuts will be your meats."

Anonymous

Flaxseed	Pumpkin	Sesame	Squash
			Sunflower

Herbs, Fresh and Dried

Add to salads, Essene breads, vegetable loaves, croquettes

Bay	Celery	Oregano	Sage
Cayenne	Marjoram	Peppermint	Sweet Basil

Sea Plants

Sea plants are extraordinarily full of the minerals and trace elements our population is so lacking. More and more, scientists are realizing the vital role they play in maintaining health.

For instance, sea plants provide an abundance of iodine needed for the thyroid gland's function. Being naturally chelated, it is readily utilized by the thyroid gland. Much of today's obesity is caused by insufficient iodine in the diet.

We notice not only increased energy from eating sea plants, but rapid growth of hair and nails.

Dulse	Kelp	Nori	Spirulina Algae
Hijiki			Wakame

Seasoning Seeds

Cardamon	Celery	Dill	Peppercorns
Caraway	Chia	Papaya (dried and ground)	Poppy

Weeds

Weeds contain far more nutrition than their purposely cu
vated progeny. They are excellent for use in salads, tacos, sauc
seasonings and chopped in Essene breads.

Bamboo Shoot	Chickweed	Dock, Yellow	Shepherd's
Bracken	Corn Lily (early	Endive	Purse (early
Bulrush	leaf)	Hollyhock	leaf)
Burdock	Cress (Land	Lambsquarter	Tansy (early
Cactus, Nopal	Cress,	Maple	leaf)
Cattail (stem,	Peppergress)	Onion, wild	Queen Anne's
early spring)	Dandelion	Sheep Sorrel	Lace
	Dock, Curley		Wild Lettuce
			Watercress

Zany, Zestful Flours, Powders and Granules

These foods not only have many uses but great nutritional value,
especially brewer's yeast and bee pollen which can be used in
recipes. Agar-agar, a sea plant product, can be used to make con-
gealed fruit and vegetable salads. Arrowroot, slippery elm and
flaxseed meal are thickeners. Other powders such as soy, rice and
the brans are good to roll in or sprinkle over fruit cookies and
sweets. Carob powder with its chocolate-like flavor, is used in the
same way chocolate and cocoa are used without any harmful, toxic
effects.

Agar-Agar	Brewer's Yeast	Rice Bran	Soy Powder
Arrowroot	Flaxseed Meal	Rice Flour	Wheat Bran
Powder	Carob Powder	(whole)	Wheat Grass
Bee Pollen	(raw)	Slippery Elm	Powder
	Oat Flour		

Edible Flowers and Blossoms

For garnish and for flavoring to your salads

Apple	Geranium	Orange	Spearmint
Chamomile	Gladiolus	Blossoms	Squash
Chive	Grape Leaves	Pansy	Strawberry
Chrysanthemum	Lavender	Primrose	Flowers
Crabapple	Marigold	Quince	Strawberry
Dandelion	Milkweed	Raspberry	Leaves
Petals	Mulberry	Leaves	Sweet Potato
Elderberry	Nasturtium Leaf,	Rose Petals	Thyme
Fuchsia	green seeds,	Rosehips	Tiger Lily Pods
Garlic	flowers	Rosemary	Wild Mustard
		Sage	Violet
		Sorrel	

Where to Buy

e United States, consumers of natural food staples
:ooperatives (co-ops). By checking your telephone
e Chamber of Commerce for such an organization,
you can find out if there is such a store in your area.

Co-ops are excellent sources of whole grains, seeds for eating and for sprouting, legumes (dry peas, beans, etc.), nuts, herbs, yeast, dried sea plants, honey, brewer's yeast, molasses, cold pressed (bulk) oils and other staples. Many even have fresh produce, organically grown. When and if you buy the bulk oils, be sure and smell the oil before buying to make sure it is not rancid.

Some grocery stores and supermarkets are now featuring bulk barrels of legumes and some seeds and/or grains. Nearly all carry hulled and unhulled sunflower seed.

Health food stores carry a wide variety of natural, unprocessed foods. Some larger ones offer staples in bulk. They also carry grinders, choppers, mills, juicers, graters, etc.

In agricultural areas and states, there are independent natural food stores that sell many or all of the basic foods for the customer on an all-natural regimen of nutrition. They usually carry locally-grown, organic vegetables and fruits in season. Many offer prices comparable to the cooperatives.

In large cities there is usually an oriental food store, Chinese and/or Japanese, that offers a wide variety of edibles such as dried foods, herbs, sea plants and soy foods — tofu, soy cheeses, soy sauce (buy only the naturally aged), tamari and the like. We suggest you include a get-acquainted trip to such a store. The storekeeper will be most helpful in instructing you in different, natural and nutritious foods. It's a whole new adventure.

In rural areas all over the country there are the familiar farmers co-ops, feed & grain stores and elevators. If you can buy untreated grain suitable for sprouting from them, you'll usually pay a far lower price than elsewhere.

If none of these sources are in your area, you may order by mail from firms who specialize in this service. In the Appendix you'll find a list of sources located all over the United States.

How To Learn What Foods And Substances Are Good For You

*"Let the mind and spirit soar. The body knows
how to take care of itself."*

S.A. Mitts

The Body Language Test for Food Allergies

The sign at the nursery read: DON'T COMPOST YOUR POTTING SOIL IN A PLASTIC CONTAINER.

Smaller print explained the mystery: earthworms can't live in plastic, no matter how well ventilated it is. If they can't escape, they die. By contrast, soil composted in metal cans offers no problem.

What tells the worm that plastic is poisonous to him? It is the cells of his body. They cannot perform normally because of constant *gassing-off* of the toxic plastic. His environmental bio-warning system tells him to leave the plastic at once.

In humans this bio-warning mechanism or system is called Body Language. The body tells what is good or bad for it, not the mind. The mind is too conditioned by conscious learning and education, by social and environmental conditioning, by ecological altering of sensory perceptions, by pollution sensitivities both external and ingested, to discern on contact, what harms or helps.

By a very simple test, the body, without any conscious effort of the mind, can indicate what is good and what is bad for it for optimal functioning.

Here is the test.

The person to be tested (the testee) stands and extends the right arm straight out, fist tightly clenched. The person who does the testing (the tester), with one hand on the testee's wrist, pulls down

on the extended arm while the testee resists as much as possible.

Keeping in mind the strength felt in the extended arm, the tester then puts some object like a soft plastic bottle in the testee's left hand. Again the testee extends the right arm, makes it rigid and clenches the fist. Again the tester pulls down on the testee's arm. If the testee's arm is easily pulled down despite all efforts to offer as much resistance as in the trial test of strength, the testee is allergic to the plastic. His body is weakened by contact with the plastic that is known to be toxic. For maximum strength and freedom from the fatigue factor, he should stay away from (soft) plastics.

A double-check can be made on the soft plastic bottle.

The testee presses the end of the little finger to the end of the thumb of the left hand with all the strength that can be applied. The tester tries to pull the finger and thumb apart, thus testing the strength of the testee's hand. Now the tester places the plastic bottle in the testee's right hand while the testee presses together the thumb and little finger of the left. The tester tries to pull the thumb and finger apart. If done so fairly easily (as against pulling them apart with great difficulty before), the testee's body is allergic to (soft) plastic.

The test was conducted on one patient by another patient in the presence of the doctor who taught us how to do the testing. Here's what the doctor had patients John and Mike to do. John was the tester, Mike the testee.

1. Mike extended his right arm straight out from his shoulder, his fist clenched, his arm rigid.

2. John tested the strength of Mike's arm by pulling down on it at the wrist after he said, "Resist me." This showed John how much strength was in Mike's arm. He had to exert considerable effort to pull Mike's arm down.

3. Into Mike's left hand, relaxed at his side, was placed a polyester sock.

4. Mike again made his extended right arm rigid and clenched his fist to resist John's trying to pull it down.

5. John had little trouble pulling Mike's arm down this time. Mike's body was weakened by contact with the polyester, a toxic material. In the present day parlance, Mike was "allergic" to polyester.

To double-check the result of the test, the doctor taught John and Mike the other way to do the same test.

1. Mike pressed the tip of his little finger to the tip of his thumb of his right hand as hard as he could. His empty left hand was

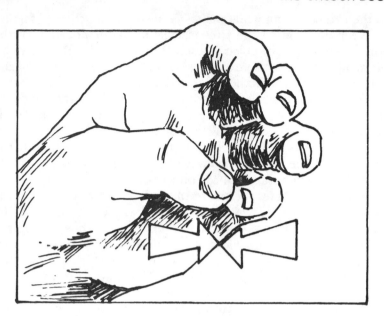

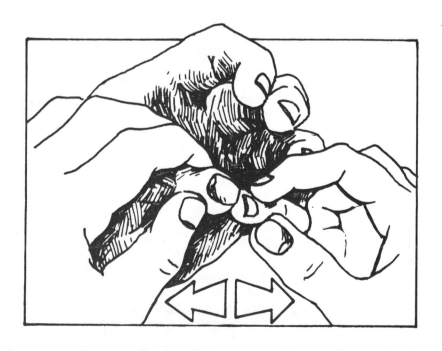

relaxed at his side.

2. With difficulty, John pulled the thumb and finger apart. Mike had formidable strength in his fingers.

3. Mike again received the polyester sock in his left hand while he pressed his right finger and thumb together.

4. John pulled Mike's little finger and thumb apart with little effort.

5. Again Mike's strength was weakened by contact with polyester.

The doctor gave two small objects to John to do another test on Mike, this time a blind test.

1. Mike extended his arm, fist clenched.

2. John tested the strength in Mike's arm by grasping the wrist and pulling down on it. There was formidable strength in the arm.

3. Into Mike's left hand, held palm up, slightly back of him and out of his sight, John laid the two small objects.

4. Mike again made his arm rigid and clenched his fist to resist John's testing of his strength.

5. John had little trouble pulling Mike's arm down.

(The doctor then showed Mike the two vitamin tablets John had laid in Mike's hand, vitamins the doctor thought of prescribing. But with Mike's body showing an allergic response, he, of course, did not prescribe them.)

The doctor had John test Mike on kelp tablets, this time using the finger-thumb method. Mike was deficient in several minerals and the doctor wanted not only to know if Mike was allergic to kelp, but how many tablets he should take. He cautioned John to be very careful in assessing Mike's strength before testing the kelp. This test could have been done blind but the doctor chose to have it done open, using the little finger-to-thumb method.

1. Mike pressed his little finger to his thumb (right hand).

2. John had difficulty pulling them apart.

3. John put one kelp tablet in Mike's left hand.

4. Mike again pressed his finger against his thumb.

5. John found the strength in Mike's hand unchanged.

6. John put another kelp tablet in Mike's hand and found the strength in Mike's thumb and finger greater.

7. John put the third tablet in Mike's left hand and found even greater strength in the thumb-pressed-against-finger of the right hand.

8. John put the fourth kelp tablet in Mike's left hand and could hardly pull the thumb and finger of the right hand apart, so great

was the strength.

9. John placed the fifth kelp tablet in Mike's left hand and found that the finger-thumb pressure of the right hand was very weak.

Comment: According to this "body language message," the proper dosage of kelp for Mike was four tablets (taken with meals).

John did a few more tests on Mike, part of the time using Mike's left arm or hand for the strength testing. (In testing several things at one session, one should alternate the hand and arm used for strength-testing to avoid undue tiring.)

Later at home, the two young men continued the testing at intervals. Mike's favorite vegetables were corn and peas, but he had noticed that he felt sluggish after eating peas. When John did a blind test of the two vegetables by laying a few of first one then the other in Mike's palm, he found that the strength in Mike's hand and arm was greatly diminished when holding the peas.

Mike learned through Body Language Testing that he was allergic to peas, peanuts, cooked starches (cereal grains, potatoes, rice), mango, carob, beef, pork, chicken and turkey, plus such over-the-counter drugs as aspirin and Tums, and his favorite brand of toothpaste. He was allergic to scented soap and household cleaners, polyethylene (car upholstery) and synthetic rubber, besides the polyester and soft plastics. By eliminating all those things in his home, he feels great and is over the illnesses he suffered as the result of his many allergies and sensitivities. With his much improved health and diet, he is able to tolerate the everyday toxins he encounters away from home if not exposed to them for too long a time.

Anyone can learn to conduct these tests, provided common sense and a few guidelines are observed.

1. Do the testing in private, free from distraction.

2. Plan to test only a few things at a session.

3. Do not continue testing immediately after the testee is found to be allergic to something. The fatigue of the arm or finger-thumb might carry over to another test and affect the results.

4. Even though the testee does not test allergic, do not test more than three things in a row because the fatigue in the arm and/or hand may alter the test results.

5. Testing is best done by adult members of the family or close friends.

6. In testing children, great care must be taken in explaining the rules of the test, then in observing the degree of strength in the child's hand and arm in both phases of the test.

7. In the case of an ill person, test only one thing at a session. The thumb-little-finger test is advisable.

8. If the food or object to be tested cannot be held by the hand of the testee, the hand can be placed against or on top of it.

9. Gases can be tested by having the testee breathe fresh air during the preliminary appraisal of the strength of arm or fingers. While he breathes the gas, the strength of his fingers or arm are tested.

10. The Body Language Test for allergies is not a parlor game. It is a serious, highly useful test for indicating why the body may be suffering from weaknesses, dysfunction, fatigue or illness.

Note: Both the tester and the testee *must remain sober* during the testing. Smiling alters results.

Before anyone can prescribe a proper diet for another or for himself/herself, he/she needs to know what foods may cause a problem. If the body is sensitive to a food (allergic), that food becomes a poison that the system has to cope with. If the liver is healthy and can detoxify the unusable food, no particular problem is noted. But if the liver cannot detoxify the offending food, the body has a problem which may show up as indigestion, grogginess, headache, constipation, skin condition, arthritis and so on ad infinitum.

Use the Body Language Test carefully to reveal offending foods. The body does not lie. Avoid eating any food that cuts the body's energy as indicated by the test. After a few weeks, try eating the food all alone if you do not have full confidence in the Body Language Test and see if you feel good after eating it. If not, then you know to leave it alone.

Periodically (usually six months), we retest a food that we were sensitive to. Once in awhile, we find one that no longer gives a problem. In such a case, we find it advisable to eat it only once in awhile.

Theoretically, the body should not be sensitive to any foods if it is receiving optimal nutrition. However, in our present society there are many extenuating circumstances that alter the health and needs of many of us. There are pollutants that may cause us to need more vitamins, plus the fact that every person on earth is an individual. No two of us are alike. The human body is extremely complicated. Science does not yet know why some can eat a perfectly good, highly nutritious, pure, natural food and some can't. But the body will tell us if we consult it. Remember that it tells the truth. Follow the rules and use the Body Lanugage Test to know that truth.

How To Combine Foods For Good Digestion And Moderate Eating

"And every man that striveth for the mastery
is temperate in all things."
                                    1 Corinthians 9:25

"We are what we eat," is a cliche that's been around a long time. No doubt it was true when someone first said it. To make the cliche apply to today's population, however, we would have to say, "We are what we eat if we digest it." In other words, we are what we digest and absorb.

No matter how optimal our diet, it cannot give us maximum health, energy and well-being if our digestive system is faulty. Many biochemists, physiologists, physicians and nutritionists agree that somewhere in an impaired digestive system, degenerative disease has its beginnings. Because of this impairment, some nutrients are not getting to certain cells in the weakest, most vulnerable parts of the body and as a result, these cells cannot maintain or repair themselves. Degeneration starts.

Carbohydrates (starches and sugars), proteins and fats are digested differently and at various rates of time. In fact, most of the digestion of one may take place in a completely different part of the digestive system than another.

For instance, starches are mainly digested in the mouth by a digestive juice called ptalin in the saliva. Its flow is stimulated by the act of chewing. When this largely digested starch is swallowed, stomach digestion continues slightly for an hour or two before the starches are passed on to the small intestine for the beginning of absorption.

Proteins are chewed and mixed in the mouth with a special

digestive juice of the saliva which stimulates the production of hydrochloric acid in the stomach. This strong acid starts protein digestion by further breaking down the food protein to amino acids in preparation for final digestion and absorption in the intestines.

Relatively little digestion of fats takes place before reaching the intestines. Since fats inhibit the secretion of gastric juices, the presence of oil or other fat in the stomach slows down the digestion of the different foods present that would otherwise have digested quite readily. Fat lowers the amount of appetite secretion poured into the stomach and the amount of other digestive juice secretions. This in turn lowers the activity of the gastric glands and lessens the amount of pepsin and hydrochloric acid produced in the stomach. It is understandable that digestion of a meal that includes fats may be slowed two or three hours.

Having some idea of the time and place required to digest the greater part of the three food groupings, we can begin to understand the basics of right and wrong food combinations.

Physiologists agree that the mouth, the stomach and the intestines secrete special digestive juices or modification of juices for each kind of food. When we eat the complex mixtures society now dictates, we put a strain on the digestive system, impairing its function. This custom more often than not leads to overeating. The seriousness of ingesting too much food cannot be overemphasized. Since simpler, smaller meals are more easily digested, they are more health-giving.

For example, fats inhibit and slow down the digestion of protein. However, since uncooked green vegetables counteract the inhibiting effect of fat, they are good to eat with a protein that has unavoidable fat in it such as seeds, nuts and flesh marbled with fat. The meal should consist of a large amount of greens, preferably in a raw salad.

Note: Eat fats and proteins at separate meals.

Proteins and sugars eaten together spell trouble even though the eater sees no immediate overt and adverse reaction. Remember that the sugars —brown raw artificially colored and white sugar, syrups, honey, sweet fruits, lactose, etc. —undergo practically no digestion in the mouth or stomach and are digested in the small intestine. When eaten alone, they stay in the stomach as little as twenty minutes. But when eaten with other foods like starches and the slower digesting proteins and fats, they are so delayed they tend to ferment.

Note: Eat sugars and proteins at separate times.

When starches are eaten, little hydrochloric acid is secreted in the stomach. When proteins are eaten, much hydrochloric acid is produced. If starches and proteins go into the stomach together, they cannot both be well accommodated. The starches are delayed, and the proteins haven't enough hydrochloric acid. The starches may reach the small intestine in a stage of fermentation which can cause gas, and the proteins go into the intestine without enough stomach digestion for eventual absorption into the blood stream. Such faulty utilization of protein (amino acids at this point) may cause flatulence, lower intestinal gas and malabsorption in spite of the fact that the person concerned may not have overeaten.

Note: Eat starches and proteins separately.

Acidic foods and proteins eaten together create another problem. Fruit acid inhibits the production of gastric secretions, notably pepsin which is necessary in the digestion of proteins. When not enough pepsin is produced, putrefaction of the protein food results.

Note: Eat acids and proteins separately.

The acid of acid fruits and vegetables destroys ptalin and the enzyme lipase in the saliva of the mouth necessary for the proper digestion of starch. Custom has set the pattern of orange, grapefruit or tomato juice at the beginning of a toast, pancake or cereal breakfast. With little or no ptalin or lipase secreted in the saliva of the mouth, the starches have to depend on enzymes from the pancreas to digest them, putting a strain on the all-important organ which may eventually lead to overwork and failure.

Note: Eat acid and starch foods separately.

Other inadvisable food combinations are starches and starches, and proteins and proteins. Remember that the healthy digestive system is vastly, complexly adaptive to match the proper kind of gastric secretions to digest each individual food. Potatoes and bread, both starches, each requires its own special secretions for good digestion, as do different kinds of proteins, such as flesh and seeds. The inadvisability of eating two or more starches at a time, or two or more proteins at a time lies in the amount ingested. One usually overeats.

Note: Eat one starch at a time.
　　　　Eat one protein at a time.

There are a few foods that should never be taken with any other foods. This is especially true of watermelon, cantaloupe and milk. In our experience working with countless people and observing many more in health spas and institutes, we have encountered none who could not tolerate watermelon when eaten alone. Milk, if one can digest it (allergists and other physicians say at least 50% of us can't), should also be taken alone. A meal of just milk if you insist. Man is the only creature in nature that continues to take a suckling's food into and through adulthood.

Note: Eat watermelon alone.
Eat cantaloupe alone.
Drink milk alone.

The following tables show food combinations that are compatible. Any other combinations place undue stress on the digestive system.

Food Combining Table

"To live up to the health ideal is to eat one food at a meal."

Ben Pauling

Proteins		**Green Vegetables**
		Lettuce
		Eggplant
		Spinach
Nuts		Green Peas
Cereals (whole grain)		Green Beans
Seeds	good	Carrots
Dried Peas and Beans	with	Radishes
Sea Foods		Broccoli
Flesh Foods		Cauliflower
Dairy Foods		Fresh Corn
		Sprouts
		Summer Squash
		etc.

Starches

Cereals (whole grain)
Chestnuts
Dried Peas and Beans
Jerusalem Artichokes
Potatoes
Pumpkin
Winter Squash

good
with

Green Vegetables

Asparagus
Beans (green)
Beets (roots and tops)
Broccoli
Cabbage
Carrots
Celery
Chard
Kale
Lettuce
Sprouts
Summer Squash
etc.

Acid Fruits

Citrus Fruits
Cranberry
Pineapple
Plums (sour)
Pomegranates
Strawberries
Sour Fruits (raspberries,
blackberries, loganberries,
currents, sour cherries)

fair
to
poor
with

Sub-Acid Fruits

Apples
Apricots
Blueberries
Cherries (sweet)
Grapes
Mangoes
Peaches
Pears

Sweet Fruits

Bananas
Dates
Figs
Prunes (sweet)
Raisins
Papaya
Persimmons

fair
with

Sub-Acid Fruits

Apples
Apricots
Blueberries
Cherries (sweet)
Grapes
Mangoes
Peaches
Pears
Sprouts
etc.

Note: All fruits go well with sprouts (in moderation) since the starch in the seeds has largely been converted to the simple sugars that are also found in fruits. Protein in sprouts has been converted to amino acids and as such is predigested.

Fats (solid and oil)		Green Vegetables
		Alfalfa Sprouts
Avocado*		Asparagus
Butter	good	Cauliflower
Corn Oil	with	Brussel Sprouts
Lard†		Chard
Olive Oil		Leeks
Peanut Oil		Mushrooms
Seed Oils		Peppers (sweet)
Suet†		Soybean Sprouts
		Tomato**

* Avocado may be eaten with all foods except proteins, melons and milk.
** Tomato combines well with protein and green vegetables.
† These foods are not recommended. They are included only for clarity.

Note: Melons (watermelon, cantaloupe, honeydew, etc.) are best eaten alone.

Sprouts are so varied and special a food they need their own table. Take the legumes, a protein-starch food in the dry form. When sprouted several days, the proteins are broken down to amino acids (which makes them come under the classification of predigested). The starches are mainly converted to sugars.

Grains are also a protein-starch food which is difficult to digest in the cooked form. In sprouts of 1 to 3 days, the protein is converted to amino acids and the starch to simple sugars (such as fructose, glucose, etc.).

Sprout Combining Table

Protein

Nuts
Seeds
Soy Cheese, etc.

Sprouted Legumes

Adzuki Bean
Alfalfa   good
Clover   with
Garbanzo (chickpea)
Lentil
Mung
Pea
Soybean

Green Vegetables

Lettuce
Turnips
Green Limas, etc.

Starches

Dry Beans, Peas
Potatoes, etc.

Sub-Acid and Sweet* Fruits

Prunes
Bananas, etc.

* In moderation. Such a combination encourages overeating.

Green Vegetables

Romaine Lettuce
Parsnips
Zucchini, etc.

Sprouted Cereal Grains

Barley   good
Buckwheat   with
Corn
Millet
Oats
Rice
Rye
Triticale
Wheat

Proteins*

Seeds
Nuts
Soy Cheese

Sub-Acid and Sweet* Fruits

Peaches
Pears
Persimmons, etc.

* In moderation. Such a combination encourages overeating.

GOOD

POOR

Proteins

* All flesh foods
and dairy foods

Starches

GOOD

POO

* *Flesh foods and dairy foods*
not recommended.

Avocado goes with all foods but
proteins and melons.

COMBINING CHART

POOR

POOR

POOR

POOR

POOR

FAIR

FAIR

Fruits (Sweet)

Fruits (Sub-Acid)

Fruits (Acid)

Sprouts

Green
Vegetables

Tomato mixes with fruits and vegetables.

Melons - eat alone.

Sprouted cereal grains are so versatile they can, in moderation, be eaten with almost anything. Remember that the protein of the cereal grains has been converted to amino acids, making it "predigested," and the starch has been largely converted to simple sugars.

The Essene breads made with chopped vegetables or with nuts and dried fruit, warmed and brushed with a trace of softened butter make a wonderfully satisfying, delicious and ideal meal. However, the vegetable Essene breads go well with avocado or a vegetable salad or raw soup, and the fruit-nut Essene breads go well with a fruit salad or a dried fruit spread.

The reader will notice that cereal grains and dried legumes (peas, beans, etc.) are listed under both *proteins* and *starches*. They *contain* proteins and starches, two food substances we are advised not to deliberately combine. The truth of the matter is both cereal grains and legumes in the *cooked* state are hard to digest. Unless the cooked cereal grains are eaten alone, the starch they contain tends to ferment and the protein putrifies, giving the eater heartburn or stomach disorder and foul-smelling stools. And cooked dried legumes can cause the same symptoms with the added distress of lower intestinal gas.

By sharp contrast, sprouted cereal grains and legumes cause none of these problems. One simply has to try them to experience that great difference.

But before we concern ourselves too much with eating, we should consider fasting — a custom that is as old as the history of man. Fasting was practiced in all ancient civilizations. Man recognized the value of a period without food to allow the body to cleanse itself of impurities.

Even animals know to fast to regain and keep their health. Nature itself provided fasts for man in the seasons of the year. By spring, when food supplies were gone, man's body benefited by a lean diet that allowed his body to rid itself of toxins accumulated during the inactive winter.

In talking to the disciples, Jesus said *when* ye fast, (not *if* ye fast), taking for granted that the established, wholesome and necessary-for-good-health custom of fasting would continue.

So *when* you fast, consider these pointers — after you check with your therapist or physician to make sure it is all right for you to fast:

1. Choose a time when you can be quiet, away from the mainstream of your social and work life. A long weekend serves well.

2. To extend the time, should you need it, try not to eat on the last

day of your work week, but drink plenty of water (preferably distilled). Some fasting therapists and physicians say to lick a little salt now and then all through the fast to help keep you from dehydrating too quickly and losing energy.

3. Rest as much as possible during your fast.

4. Explain briefly to your family or a close friend about your fast well before you start it. Then do not discuss it with anyone. Talk about it as litle as possible to your family or friends.

5. Your second day of fasting may be very difficult, with a general feeling of malaise which may lessen the third day. The fourth day you will probably feel better. If at all possible, go through the day without eating. Usually by that time one feels quite good and has no difficulty resisting the urge to eat. Much of eating is habit or food addiction.

6. Break the fast with something easy to digest. Fruit in season, only one kind at a meal, as for instance, cantaloupe or pears (peeled unless organic).

7. Continue for several meals with some kind of fruit, then a vegetable salad with sprouts. After your fast, it will be much easier to go on and stay on a transitional diet.

How And What To Eat And Drink

"Chew your liquids and drink your foods."
The Mahatma Gandhi

Most Americans are victims of the pernicious habit of eating too fast. We also eat too much. Fast eating almost invariably leads to eating too much.

They are both bad. Eating too fast may be a result of habit, hurry, pressure, stress, anxiety, faulty appestat and/or a host of emotional conditions. For whatever reason the end result — eating too fast, "gulping" or "bolting" food — means not enough chewing. Some physicians say to chew your bites of food 25 times. Others say 45. For most foods the number of "chomps" necesary to pulverize and thoroughly mix the food with saliva is more like 75. Some foods like almonds take more. Two almond kernels are not converted into a liquid (cream) until after some 130 chomps! And that's with a complete set of grinding molars. Don't take our word for it. Try it. You'll eat far *fewer* almonds and get far *more* nutrition. Think of the food and the body energy you'll save.

We once conducted an experiment, the first half of which was unknown to the two young men we tested. Since each enthusiastically agreed to a delicious meal of fresh peaches and almonds, we set them down to 6 medium sized peaches and 20 almond kernels. The two eaters were nearly the same weight, height and age.

In 16 minutes one ate six peaches and all 20 almonds. In 22 minutes the other ate 18 almonds and five peaches. The first one burped about three minutes before finishing. Both young men reported belching a time or two a little after the meal.

Days later the same two young men were invited to eat the same delicious meal again. This time we told them to eat all they wanted and to count each bite, eating first one kind of food, then the other, and chew until the food was thoroughly broken down and mixed with saliva. The faster eater started with peaches, chewing each bite 35 to 50 times before all food was completely swallowed. He ate the almonds last, chewing each 2 almonds 122 times before all "creamed" almonds were swallowed. He ate only 5 of the peaches and 15 of the almonds. His eating time was 23 minutes.

The other young man ate the almonds first, chewing about 136 times for each bite. The peaches required an average of 51 times for each bite. He ate 12 almonds and 4 peaches. His eating time was 26 minutes.

Neither belched during or after the meal. They attributed this fact, in defense of their eating habits, to the unusualness of the meal!

Later they reported "feeling great" after the second meal and energetic all during their afternoon lab work. (They were both in their last year of medical school.) They did not become sleepy, sluggish and drowsy as they so often did for a couple of hours after their conventional cafeteria lunch.

From a purely economic outlook, they illustrate a point that has since been demonstrated by many. The faster eater, by eating much slower, ate 17% fewer almonds and 10% fewer peaches, an average of 13% less food. The slower eater who ate 13½% less food than the other in the first meal, cut his second, without intentionally doing so, by 20% fewer peaches and 33% fewer almonds, an average of 26½% less food consumed.

In spite of their being greatly impressed, they didn't succeed in changing their eating habits soon. The faster eater took about 3½ years, the slower one about two.

We realize this isolated experiment on only two subjects, as well matched as they were, is no conclusive bit of research. It was conducted to draw a problem — physical, social and economical — to two rather opinionated young men, and it worked, as it has on any number of unrecorded cases. We only suggest that you try it on yourself and possibly on your family. The foods may vary, but those tested the two times must be the same and in easily measurable quantities. Don't announce the rules of the test or even that you're testing to your family. Prejudices and extenuating circumstances can enter in too readily. Simply conduct the test in curiosity and serious fun.

It's an easy way to "down" food costs and "up" digestion and health.

Rules and regulations are both bad words in our socially free and permissive society. But to help us learn health discipline — and that is what firstly, health and nutrition is all about — we might do well to see a list of rules. They help us focus on the minimum essentials, the foundation blocks that we start building our health on.

1. Give thanks to God for the food He provided.
2. Eat slowly.
3. Chew extremely well.
4. Eat only when calm.
5. Don't eat if in a hurry. (You won't starve if you miss a meal. If you feel you are starving, or you've discovered you have low blood sugar, or you are a food-aholic, you need to read some books like *Psycho-Nutrition* by Carlton Fredericks, *Be Your Own Doctor* by Ann Wigmore or *Sprout For The Love Of Everybody* by Viktoras Kulvinskas.)
6. Avoid drinking water or other liquids with a meal. Liquids dilute saliva, discourage sufficient mastication and inhibit digestion. If you insist on drinking water with a meal, it should be well between bites and not washing down some dry or partially chewed bite.
7. Cultivate pleasant conversation or no conversation at a meal. Some like to have soft, soothing, slow-tempoed music playing.
8. Eat simply. One or two foods at a time if possible. At least start simplifying your meals now and have as your goal a mono-food or duo-food diet, or a regimen that limits meals to four different foods.
9. If a burp surfaces toward the end of a meal, stop eating. Any more will be too much. Don't make a garbage can of your digestive tract. Stop even though you leave something on your plate. It will make good compost for your growing soil.

What to eat usually gets us into an argument. But since words on paper can't talk back, we'll risk bringing up points of contention. We'll simply list the basic foods and drinks we've found to be health-giving.

Foods
1. All natural.
2. Organically grown.
3. Pure soap-washed and rinsed, or soda-washed then vinegar rinsed. (Soda neutralizes acids in poison sprays and dips, vinegar counteracts alkalies.)
4. As much as possible, fresh, whole fruits and vegetables. Prepare only enough to eat immediately. For instance, don't peel

and slice cantaloupe to store in the refrigerator. Vitamins on the cut edges may be lost, especially Vitamin C, with exposure to air (oxygenation).

5. Eat only freshly ground nuts and seeds. Grind only what is to be eaten immediately. Freeze any left over.

6. Eat the mostly whole fruits and vegetables instead of juices made from them. Vitamin loss in juices is rapid. In a glass of freshly extracted orange juice, for instance, 30% of Vitamin C is lost in ten minutes. Juices are usually gulped down and not "chewed". This contributes to our appalling habit of always having to have something to drink, day and night. The custom is unfortunately perpetrated by advertising and by restaurants. Note the number of pictures in such media you have seen where some character is holding a cup, glass or stein of some drink in his hand.

7. Eat mostly or all raw foods. Your thirst will go down, your taste for all kinds of beverages will gradually disappear and your bank account will stop taking the beating it now suffers.

8. Eat fewer and fewer spices, condiments, sauces and strong flavorings such as onion, garlic and cayenne. You'll gradually lose your taste for them as you start cutting down.

9. Eat no more often than every four hours to give your stomach a rest. It takes the average stomach about four hours to digest a meal.

10. Eat nothing between meals. Feeling the need for food every little while spells trouble. A healthy person can skip a meal with no ill effects.

11. Eat only a small amount if and when eating before bed. What to eat at that time is controversial. Each person should experiment to see what food does not keep sleep away. When we feel the need of food before retiring, Elizabeth takes in moderation sub-acid or acid fruit — blueberries, prunes, plums, peaches, apples, etc.; Elton a few black or English walnuts. We are all different!

12. Eat frozen foods only if fresh are not available.

13. Eat dried fruits and vegetables when fresh or frozen ones are not available. Dried foods have no Vitamin C. They are highly concentrated and need extra chewing if reconstituted in the mouth. It is best to soak them overnight in pure water.

14. Eat freshly shelled nuts. (We buy our yearly supply of nuts as each variety is harvested and store them in the deep freeze as most people store a winter's supply of meat.)

15. Eat only unsulfured, sugarless dried fruits — the dark brown scroungy-looking ones.

16. Eat quantities of leafy green vegetables unless you have arrived, through excellent health, at the ultimate fruitarian diet.

17. Eat to live in health — mental alertness, physical strength and vigor, emotional stability and contentment, spiritual enlightenment.

Dollar Savers, Penny Stretchers And Other Very Special Foods

"Beloved, I wish above all things that thou mayest prosper in health, even as the soul prospereth."

III John 2

Some foods are very special because of their unusually high nutritional qualities. Others are noteworthy for their low price tag, their versatility and their deliciousness. And some are so unusual as to be endowed with all these blessings.

In alphabetical order we are listing these foods — none new, many ages old — that have been all too neglected, overlooked, controversial or out-of-fashion. These foods can contribute the lion's share to restoring your health, maintaining it and saving you money.

Adzuki Beans are sprouting beans quite similar to the popular and widely grown mung bean but cost half as much (co-ops and natural food stores). They taste remarkably the same, but are even richer in nutrients than mung beans. The adzuki is a little more chewy and if cooked, requires from eight to ten minutes instead of three to four. Adzuki beans can easily be one of your budget staples.

Alfalfa belongs to the legume family. Alfalfa is one of the most amazing of foods for economy, nutrition and the exquisite, delicate taste of its sprouts and the tea made from steeping its seeds. In Mexico, the green leaves of the full grown alfalfa plant are included in a green drink tonic made of any combination of leafy green vegetables. Because its roots may go to a hundred feet deep, the plant is full of the earth's minerals. Besides being high in Vitamins

A, B-complex and C, it also abundantly contains D, E, G, K and U. It is rich in calcium, iron and phosphorus and has all essential amino acids.

Agar-agar, a dried extract from sea plants, provides minerals and acts as a natural laxative. It is used as a congealant in making molded salads and as a thickener. A complete food, it is a blessing to the vegetarian who wishes to make gourmet desserts and fruit candies. (One teaspoon dissolved in ½ cup hot, not boiling, water, for molded salad. Two to three times as much for making fruit "finger" confections and treats.)

Buckwheat is a vegetable (not a cereal grain), and has so many uses, a complete uncook book of recipes could be written about it. Mild in flavor, it can serve as a cereal, bread, pancake, pie crust, main dish, or salad, as well as be included in recipes from soup to nuts. Sprout it for all those uses. (Either in a jar — a bit difficult since the soak and rinse water is mucilaginous — or by damp paper towel method.) Grow the buckwheat lettuce in an inch of soil in a tray for the tenderest, most succulent of salad greens at a cost of only pennies per tray. In every form, buckwheat will give you full nutrition (vitamins, minerals, complete protein, enzymes) for very little money.

Carob (raw), is that highly nutritious food St. John lived on. It is sweet and has a flavor similar to chocolate without any of the distressful side effects. Roasted carob, which looks and tastes like cocoa, is less nutritious than raw. Ask your co-op or health food store to get the raw carob for you or order it yourself (see Appendix).

Comfrey is such a complete food man could live on it alone, just as cattle do. The growing of comfrey is encouraged by the world organizations for famine relief. It will grow in almost any climate, but best where it gets some sunshine and sufficient water. Its growth is luxuriant if kept from seeding (cut off the flowering stalk). Roots go to 90 feet deep and leaves to 39 inches long and 8 inches wide. For a start, buy a root from your nursery and grow a bunch in a small spot in yard or garden. Eat leaves in salads, steam slightly for cooked greens, or juice with other vegetables for a green drink. The root, mild in flavor, rich in all nutrients and an excellent source of carbohydrates, can be used finely chopped in a salad, ground for the base of seed-nut-meat loaves, patties, etc., fruit-carob candies and cookies.

Dried fruits should be a large part of everyone's survival storage food supply. Few nutrients are lost in the drying (dehydrating) process, Vitamin C being the main one. Fruit in the dried state is quite concentrated and sweet-tasting. However, there is no more fruit sugar in, for instance, a dried half pear or dried banana slice than in a fresh half pear or fresh banana slice. Many people say that dried fruits should be eaten very sparingly because of the high concentration of sugar. But if the eater chews each bite of dried fruit some 75 times to thoroughly reconstitute it in the mouth, or soaks the fruit in water several hours, then eats it, he will find it agrees with him as well as the fresh fruit.

If a dried fruit well reconstituted and chewed gives you a problem, then the fresh one will do the same. It is best to use the Body Language Test to determine, before eating, whether or not you have a sensitivity to the fruit.

Some people are prone to condemn dried fruits because they themselves have experienced a reaction. One cancer patient who through an all-raw diet enjoys a remission of cancer, advises all cancer patients against eating the "concentrated, sweet dried dates and fruits" because this patient got a bad reaction from eating them. The cancer flared again briefly and slightly. Yet many other cancer patients who have achieved freedom from the cancer problem find that, in moderation and with chewing sufficiently, dried fruits and dates are excellent foods for occasional consumption and for travel.

The same is true of hypoglycemics or diabetics. If they employ the Body Language Test to determine any sensitivity (allergy) they may have before eating a specific dried food, they will know definitely whether or not to eat it.

In selecting dried fruits to buy, read the labels to make sure they are not sulfured or sugared. Sulfured, preservative-treated dried fruits are the light, shiny color of fresh fruit. Choose the dark brown dehydrated bananas, pineapple, peaches, apples, apricots, etc. The natural sun or slow dehydrator drying turns fruits brown. Unsulfured prunes and figs will be dull and quite hard, but taste better than the shiny, softer sulfured ones.

Dulse (dried), or sea lettuce, should be on everyone's shelf. Twelve times more nutritious than the average vegetable, it is cheap at several dollars a pound. (It goes a long way. Wash, soak a few minutes and add to salads, Essene breads, vegetable dishes and seed-nut-meat recipes. We wash, re-dry and grind it to a coarse powder for a large-holed salt shaker which is on the table for every meal for on-the-spot seasoning.)

Peas (dried for sprouting), are a far better buy than frozen or canned both for nutrition and economy. Dry peas with sprouted shoots the length of the pea have the taste of fresh peas with several times the vitamins and enzymes. Pureed for a raw soup or warmed and seasoned for a vegetable dish or tossed into a salad, dried and sprouted peas are a favorite with children and adults. They are the cheapest way to buy peas. Look for them in co-ops and natural food stores.

Flaxseed, the long neglected seed, has all the advantages of a complete food and no disadvantages. With the highest Vitamin E content of any known seed, it also excels in complete bulk fiber (bran contains only three of the five essential bulk fibers), is mucilaginous for easy digestion, is high in complete protein and is rich in minerals and oil. This amazing seed keeps for a year or more stored in a cool place and costs half as much as the cheapest of the other seeds (sesame, sunflower, pumpkin, chia).

Cheese made with only fermec and fresh-ground flaxseed meal is delicious and keeps out of refrigeration at least 3 weeks. (Since "inventing" flaxseed cheese, we have taken it on three-week travel vacations during which it showed no change in taste or sign of spoilage.)

As a thickener, flaxseed meal can be used in everything from soups and salad dressings, to breads, candies and smoothies. Since it has seldom been used in the American diet, few people have built up a sensitivity to it. In addition to all that, it has a satisfying, nut-like flavor.

Honey, though a complete food, has only traces of all the nutrients. It is famous for its rich concentration of fruit sugars and its digestibility. A teaspoon of honey sweetens as much as two teaspoons of table sugar.

One should never eat more than a tablespoon of honey a day. We recommend no more than a teaspoonful. Eating more contributes to a problem most of us suffer from already — sugar addiction.

Kelp is a miracle food having a full complement of naturally chelated minerals in an inexpensive, palatable powder or granular form and is easy to use and contains no waste. Because it is rich in iodine which many people need for thyroid function, it alone is responsible for weight loss of many obese people who take from ¼ to one teaspoonful, two or three times a day with meals. Use kelp instead of salt in foods. Keep a shaker of it on the table.

Molasses is a controversial food because it is concentrated, sweet and, depending on the processing, may or may not contain impurities. Nevertheless, it is so mineral-rich that even a teaspoonful a day can prevent or correct mineral deficiency over a period of time.

Pollen, or bee pollen, is a highly rich B vitamin, semi-sweet substance that bees carry on their feet from the flowers to their hives. It is collected by means of a screen with mesh only large enough to admit them. As they crawl through, some of the pollen is scraped from their feet and collected in a receptacle below.

A high energy, concentrated food, pollen is controversial because of the impurities it may contain. All imported and most domestic pollens are heat dried. Bee keepers are beginning to sell their pollen raw and unprocessed. Some people taking a few half-teaspoonsful a day of locally produced pollen find their pollen allergies disappear.

Several athletes report their energy and endurance much increased when they take bee pollen.

Soy beans have, for 5,000 years, been a staple food of the Chinese. From them they still make dozens of products. Soy is a complete food.

We recommend sprouting soy beans for taste, low cost, digestibility, increased nutrition and a variety of uses. A good protein food, raw soy sprouts, cheese, soy pulp salad dressing, soy loaf, etc. can be the meat of a meal.

Tamari and **miso** are two tasty products made mainly from fermented soy, kozi and unrefined sea salt. Tomari, a liquid sauce, is a by-product of miso, a creamy paste. Both can be used as flavors and seasonings for any nonsweet foods. We especially like them for flavoring tofu, soy cheese, marinates and salad dressings (see Appendix for source).

Wheat is one of the world's most utilized cereal grains, yet because of its myriad uses in processed foods as well as breads and bakery products in the U.S., 65% of the population, according to allergists, have a sensitivity to it.

This sensitivity or allergy is often the body's inability to digest cooked starch. Fortunately, most everyone can eat sprouted wheat and wheat grass juice. In the one- to three- or four-day old sprouts, the proteins are mostly converted to amino acids (predigested) and the starches to fruit sugars, making wheat sprouts easily digested and absorbed. The juice from seven-day-old green wheat grass, high in chlorophyll and all nutrients, is also very easily digested. Wheat sprouts can be grown for pennies a day. Three cafeteria trays of wheat grass for nutritious, healing juice can be grown for the price of a pound of wheat (12¢ to 25¢).

Yeast, the primary brewer, or nutritional yeast grown on molasses, is a concentrated food rich in complete protein (all essential amino acids), the B vitamins and minerals. Another nutritional variety is called torula, a yeast grown on wood pulp, a cheaper yeast but not as tasty as the molasses-grown.

Nutritional yeast is easily digested and an excellent food to include with regular meals for deficiencies and for recovering from or preventing degenerative diseases. When bought in flake or powder form in bulk, one gets a lot of excellent nutrition for the money. Start by taking ½ to one teaspoonful with meals, gradually increasing to a tablespoonful.

Spirulina Plankton, a natural vegetable organism (algae), contains high amounts of vitamins and amino acids. It is a complete food, with especially high amounts of B_{12}, the anti-anemic factor. Rich in chlorophyll, it has great healing properties. It is claimed by many that taking as little as a teaspoonful once or twice a day raises the energy level. (See Appendix for source.)

How To Sprout And Grow Seeds And Grains In Your Kitchen

"Moisten your wheat that the angel of water may enter it...and the blessing will soon make the germ of life to sprout...then crush your grain and make thin wafers as did your forefathers."

Essene Gospel of Peace
(First Century Aramaic Manuscript)

The rapidly-spreading "new" practice of sprouting seeds has been going on in China for 5,000 years. Seed sprouting was a well-established custom when the biblical Daniel, at the court of Nebuchadnezzar, stated his preference for a diet of pulses (sprouted legumes and grains) instead of eating the rich foods and drink of the king's table (Daniel 1:12). Whether old or new, the sprouting of seeds brings delicious, nutritious and exciting foods to our table at a fraction of the cost of prepared and imported fresh foods.

The sprouting table in this chapter has the basic information you will need to start your indoor garden. It can help you to halve the food bill of your family. Without any soil, without having to wait weeks or months to harvest the seeds you plant and with very little "fuss or muss", you'll harvest your crops in a few hours or days all year round simply by removing your plants from their sprouting containers!

We think the easiest way to sprout most seeds is in wide-mouth, quart or half-gallon glass jars, covered by a circle of nylon net, cheese cloth, nylon screen wire or nylon stocking and secured with a rubber band.

Some people, however, prefer a commercially-made seed

sprouter or earthenware flower pot and saucer. In the case of the latter, cover the bottom with a circle of nylon net or something similar to keep the seeds from spilling out the drainage hole.

Select clean, disease-free, fertile seeds. Remove broken ones because they may ferment and cause spoilage among your sprouts. Wash seeds well.

Soak seeds in twice as much water as seeds. Drain off soak water and save for drinking or for watering soil-grown seeds (in the house) and houseplants or for use in tea, soups and blender beverages. This slightly discolored water is rich in nutrients.

Rinse the seeds by running water into the net-covered jar until it overflows. This flushes out the bubbles which are the beginning of fermentation. Pour water off and turn jar upside down at a 45° angle to drain yet not dry out. It also allows air to circulate in the jar.

Best temperature for sprouting is 68° to 84°. Your sprouts will do well in a warm corner of your kitchen either in a cupboard or covered with a dark cloth. We use a dish drainer set over a drip pan with a forest green dish towel spread over the upturned jars for darkness.

Sprouts such as alfalfa, clover, rye and chia should be allowed to grow two leaves. We set them in bright light or sun for greening.

Garbanzos and soy beans spoil easily unless rinsed four to six times a day. To avoid the risk of spoilage and to save time, we soak them eight hours, rinse and drain well, then put them in the refrigerator until the length desired, rinsing only once a day. They'll keep several days. (Toss a few in salads and soups.)

When sprouting the "gluey" flaxseed and hulled buckwheat seeds, we use the jar method, soaking only a couple of hours then rinsing several times a day. The mucilaginous soak water is very good for intestinal problems and colitis. It may also be used in recipes.

For some small seeds like chia, cress, mustard and radish, the paper towel method is best. (Some people prefer this method for flaxseed and buckwheat.) Wet and wring out two paper towels and line the bottom of a flat dish or pyrex pan. Plant seeds evenly over surface and cover with two layers of moist paper towels. Sprinkle to keep towels moist. When plants are about 1½ inches long, remove towels and allow sprouts to grow and green in daylight for three or four hours, sprinkling two or three times, then harvest.

The soaking time of grains is not critical. In summer they need less soak time. Some seeds like lentils and mung beans are juicier and sprout in fewer days when soaked 24 hours. The soak water should be changed at least once during that time or it will sour. Most people prefer salad lentils sprouted only two days. For juicing, five days is best.

Store sprouts in the refrigerator in a covered dish, sealed plastic bag or glass jar. They will keep four or five days.

See Sprouting Chart on the following pages.

Seeds	Sprouting Equipment	Soaking Time	Water, Rinse and Drain	Sprouting Time
Adzuki	Jar	8 hours	3 times/day	3-4 days
Alfalfa	Jar	8 hours	3 times/day	4-5 days
Almond	Paper Towels	4 hours; drain	Sprinkle 3 times/day	3-5 days
Barley	Jar	8 hours	3 times/day	3-5 days
Beans	Jar	8 hours	3 times/day	3-5 days
Buckwheat	Jar or Paper Towels	8 hours	3 times/day	2-3 days
Cabbage	Jar	8 hours	3 times/day	3-5 days
Chia	Flat bottom bowl		Sprinkle 3 times/day	4-5 days
Clover	Jar	8 hours	3 times/day	1-2 days
Corn	Jar	8 hours	3 times/day	4-8 days
Fenugreek	Jar	8 hours	3 times/day	3-4 days
Flax	Jar or Paper Towels	4 hours	4 times/day	4-5 days
Garbanzo	Jar	8 hours	4 times/day	2-3 days
Garden Cress	Jar	8 hours	3 times/day	3-4 days
Lentil	Jar	8 hours	3 times/day	3-4 days
Millet	Jar	8 hours	3 times/day	3-4 days
Mung Bean	Jar	8 hours	3 times/day	3-5 days
Mustard	Paper Towels	4 hours; drain	Sprinkle 3 times/day	3-5 days
Oat	Jar	8 hours	4 times/day	2-3 days
Pea	Jar	8 hours	3 times/day	3-4 days
Pumpkin	Jar	8 hours	3 times/day	3-4 days
Radish	Jar	8 hours	3 times/day	2-4 days
Rice	Jar	8 hours	3 times/day	3-4 days
Rye	Jar	8 hours	3 times/day	2-4 days
Sesame	Jar	8 hours	3 times/day	3-4 days
Soybean	Jar	8 hours	4-5 times/day	2-4 days
Sunflower	Jar	8 hours	2 times/day	24-36 hrs.
Triticale	Jar	8 hours	3 times/day	1-3 days
Wheat	Jar	8 hours	3 times/day	3-5 days

1. Alfalfa, clover and rye sprouts, when an inch or two long, may be greened in daylight or sunlight for two to four hours for salad greens.

2. Beans include white, black, haricot, kidney, fava, pinto, navy, lima and broad.

3. Cabbage and other members of the same botanical family - broccoli, brussel sprouts, cauliflower, collards, and kale.

4. Garbanzos are also called chickpeas and gram.

Harvest Length	Yield	Suggested Use
1"	½ c. seeds, 2 c. sprouts	Salads, sandwiches, juices
1½" to 2"	3 T. seeds, 1 qt. sprouts	Salads, juices, soups, sandwiches
⅛" to ¼"	½ c. seeds, ¾ cups	Snacks, use in almond recipes
¼"	1 c. seeds, 1 c. sprouts	Breads, soups, cereals
½" to 1½"	1 c. seeds, 4 c. sprouts	Vegetable loaves, salads
⅛" to ½"	1 c. seeds, 3 c. sprouts	Salads, cereals, cookies, breads
½" to 1"	¼ c. seeds, 1¼ c. sprouts	Salads, seasonings, sandwiches
½"/ 2 leaves	2 T. seeds, 3 c. sprouts	Soups, dips, spreads
Seed length	½ c. seeds, 1¼ c. sprouts	Salads, spreads, soups
½"	½ c. seeds, 1 c. sprouts	Soups, salads, cereals
½"	¼ c. seeds, 1 c. sprouts	Salads, vegetable loaves
1" to 2"	2 T. seeds, 1½-2 c. sprouts	Curries, spreads, salads
¼" to ½"	½ c. seeds, 1 c. sprouts	Soups, marinates, salads
1½ in. greened	1 T. seeds, 1½ c. sprouts	Slaw salads, seasoning
1"	½ c. seeds, 1 c. sprouts	Salads, soups
¼"	1 c. seeds, 3 c. sprouts	Breads, cereals
2" to 2½"	1 c. seeds, 4-5 c. sprouts	Salads, vegetable dishes
1" to 2"	1 T. seeds, ¼ c. sprouts	Salads, seasonings
¼" to ½"	1 c. seeds, 2 c. sprouts	Breads, cereals, cookies
Seed length	½ c. seeds, 1 c. sprouts	Soups, vegetable dishes
¼"	1 c. seeds, 2 c. sprouts	Snacks, salads, candy
½" to 1"	1 T. seeds, ¾ c. sprouts	Seasonings, salads
Seed length	1 c. seeds, 2½ c. sprouts	Vegetable loaves, cereals
Seed length	1 c. seeds, 2-3 c. sprouts	Breads, granola
Seed length	1 c. seeds, 1½ c. sprouts	Cheese, cookies
1"	1 c. seeds, 2-3 c. sprouts	Tofu, cheese, salads
⅛" to ¼"	1 c. seeds, 2 c. sprouts	Vegetable "meat", salads
Seed length	1 c. seeds, 2-3 c. sprouts	Breads, cereals
Seed length	1 c. seeds, 3-4 c. sprouts	

Soil-Grown Sprouts

For the most delicious and economical salad greens, free from sprays or chemicals, try growing sprouts on soil in a sunny window.

Here's how: Spread one inch of top soil mixed with peat moss (about half-and-half), and kelp powder (a tablespoon to every three or four pounds of soil) on a plastic cafeteria tray or baking pan. Sprinkle soil until moist but not saturated. Spread a cup of 24-hour sprouted, unhulled buckwheat, sunflower seed or wheat evenly over the soil. Seeds will touch each other in a single layer. Cover with another tray, a sheet of black plastic or wet newspapers for three days. The fourth day remove the cover, sprinkle with water and place in the bright light of a window. Water every day for three or four more days.

Your indoor garden will be a beautiful, solid stand of luscious green. Harvest by cutting handfuls with a sharp, serrated-edge knife. Use immediately or store in the refrigerator in covered dish, jar or sealed plastic bag. (Avoid using soft plastic refrigerator "dishes" that continuously gas-off.)

The buckwheat "lettuce" is delicate in texture and taste and delicious when eaten alone or with other vegetables in a salad. Sunflower sprouts have thick, juicy leaves, tender stems and a tasty flavor that defies description. Use both in any salads, sandwiches, green drinks, vegetable dishes, Essene breads, pizza, tacos or enchiladas.

Juice the green wheat for the most nutritious drink known. Grind the wheat grass in a meat grinder, or power grinder-juicer, press out the juice in cheesecloth or nylon net, dilute with water, soak water or fermec (pg. 151) and drink at once.

Wheat grass juice is a complete food. The chlorophyll, similar to hemoglobin, has been known for centuries for its healing qualities and as a blood cleanser. Recent research has proven that it inhibits the growth of cancer. It is full of all known vitamins and minerals, and its abundance of enzymes makes it easy to digest.

Wheat grass juice is extremely sweet. When first drinking the juice, take only a teaspoonful or two. You may feel a bit nauseous or dizzy. This will soon pass as you take the juice each day, increasing it up to two ounces. If one is suffering from any degenerative disease, two ounces three times a day taken with an optimal diet helps the body heal and cure itself. Daniel tells how King Nebuchadnezzar lost his health and his mind but being favored by heaven, was allowed to eat grass in the fields with the oxen for seven years. At the end of that time, he regained not only his health and his sanity but his kingdom as well, and was more respected than ever (Daniel 25:37).

For problems of the colon, two to four ounces of wheat grass juice is especially good as an antiseptic, cleanser and healing agent implanted in the rectum after an enema. *(Be Your Own Doctor* by Ann Wigmore).

In the 1930's and 40's, crude chlorophyll was used by several doctors and found to be very effective in fighting bacteria, improving hemoglobin and combating degenerative disease.

In recent years, chlorophyll has been found to be effective in throat sprays, breath deodorants and for anemia, to mention a few of its medicinal uses.

It is difficult to realize how full of complete, easily absorbable nutrition wheat grass and sprouts are. A number of books have been written on the subject. We especially recommend *Sprouts For The Love Of Everybody,* by Viktoras Kulvinskas. It is packed full of well-researched information every person interested in nutrition and health may want to know.

More Notes On Wheat Grass And Its Chlorophyll

"All flesh is grass and its beauty is like the flowers in the field."

Isaiah 40:6

The so-called fad for eating wheat grass is actually a custom that has been around for nearly 5,000 years. It is a matter of recorded history that the ancient Greeks, Romans and Chinese used it and paid great tribute to its curative powers. And for good reason.

From the soil, wheat takes most of the known minerals. Its roots reach down nearly 100 feet. It is one of the best foods not only for day-to-day eating but for storage for survival. Seven-day-old wheat grass is full of minerals, enzymes and vitamins — Vitamins C and A, B_{12}, D, E, K, U and, of course, all the other known B vitamins. It is a complete food — proteins, carbohydrates, fats — with such an abundance of enzymes and chlorophyll that, as far as is known, it is second only to corn which holds the record to date.

The ancients knew the value of wheat grass for the maintenance of health and curing of diseases. The moderns have researched it in laboratories to find the reasons for that effectiveness, especially since Dr. Melvin Calvin's extensive and inspired research on the chemical reactions produced by the plant in the presence of light energy, as sunlight, electric light and so on. His research and findings resulted in the Nobel Prize in 1962.

Interestingly, scientists have found that the chlorophyll molecule has the same structure as the hemoglobin (red blood cell) molecule. The difference between the two molecules is this: the center of the chlorophyll molecule is magnesium while the center of the hemoglobin molecule is iron.

The uses of wheat grass juice for nutrition and therapy are many. We list some of them here:

77

1. Wheat grass taken internally (an ounce or two, one to three times a day, 30 minutes to an hour before meals) purifies the blood; detoxifies the body; helps to eliminate mucus in the intestines; helps chelate (take out) poisonous minerals as lead, mercury and cadmium; improves energy endurance, general health and the sense of well-being; helps correct anemia; restores gray hair to its original color. It is also effective against eczema and psoriasis; helps reduce blood pressure; helps dissolve scar tissue, both externally (rubbed on) and internally; increases hormonal activity; accelerates the healing of burns; aids in alleviating constipation; nourishes the brain and nervous system; inhibits growth of cancer cells; prevents degenerative disease; improves the quality of cells and acts as a restorer of body and mind.

2. Wheat grass juice used in the oral cavities of the body is highly beneficial — as a mouthwash, throat gargle, eye wash, ear wash, sinus irrigation and vaginal douche. Wheat grass relieves toothaches and canker sores, too. Simply hold some saturated pulp on the affected part.

3. Wheat grass topical uses are many. The skin readily absorbs what is put on it. Wheat grass is very effective as a scalp tonic, rubbed in before a shampoo. It serves well as a sterilizer-healer on a sore or wound; as a skin cleanser; as a facial; even as nutrition when rubbed 20 times on the skin. (Very ill people can be "fed" through the skin.)

4. Wheat grass juice is invaluable in surviving radiation exposure. It increases resistance to X-rays and helps protect against cell destruction. Additionally, it slows down the harmful effects of air pollution and poisonous gasses like carbon monoxide.

5. Other uses of wheat grass: When traveling, take along a cellophane bag of wheat grass and chew a handful now and then, spitting out the pulp. Place a cafeteria tray or pan of growing wheat grass in front of the color TV to help protect viewers from radiation. Wheat grass growing in the house cleanses and deodorizes the air and a few blades of wheat grass defluorinates water, according to tests made by the New York City Water Department. Children grow and develop better, and older people's cells are rejuvenated when taking wheat grass juice.

6. A word or warning on the use of wheat grass juice. While it has been repeatedly established that there is nothing toxic in wheat grass, the juice can cause nausea or stomach ache when first taken. One should start with only a teaspoonful diluted with fermec or water and increase up to two ounces three times a day.

Initially, you may want to dilute with equal amounts of liquid. Always sip slowly, mixing well with the saliva. The philosophy, "If a little is good, more is better," does not apply to wheat grass juice. It is a powerful food and must be taken in respectful moderation.

7. Scientists have found that chorophyll inhibits the growth of cancer cells. Cancer cells proliferate only where there is not enough oxygen for good healthy cells. The wheat grass is high in Vitamins E and C, both of which help the cells conserve their supply of oxygen.

8. Chlorophyll green drinks can be delicious. They give a lovely "high" without any depressing "lows". Here are a few to inspire your own creativity.

Celery-Wheat Grass
    5 oz. celery juice
    1 oz. wheat grass juice
    1 oz. distilled water

Wheat Grass Pineapplade*
    4 oz. pineapple juice
    2 oz. wheat grass juice
    1 to 2 oz. distilled water

Dr. Baker's
Green Green Drink
    2 oz. comfrey juice
    2 oz. celery juice
    1 to 2 oz. wheat grass juice

Vegetable Juice Cocktail
    3 oz. carrot
    2 oz. celery
    1 oz. fermec
    1 or 2 oz. wheat grass juice

Favorite Green Drink
    2½ oz. wheat grass juice
    2 or 3 oz. fermec

Lemon Green*
    2 oz. wheat grass juice
    1 oz. lemon juice
    1 or 2 t. honey
    4 oz. distilled water

* Recommended only very occasionally. Wheat grass is a vegetable and mixes much better with vegetables.

Foraging — Food For The Taking

"The best doctors in the world are Doctor Diet, Doctor Quiet, and Doctor Merryman."
Jonathan Swift

Many of us feed our garbage cans better than ourselves and in so doing literally throw away money along with the trash. A few pertinent suggestions may help reverse the galloping trend that is leading us all to financial crippling if not disaster.

Let us start foraging for food in our kitchens and vegetable gardens. The beet, carrot, turnip and radish tops that usually get cut off and thrown in garbage cans or disposals contain the very nutrients most of us in the western world are deficient in. So when buying, say, two bunches of beets to cook for the family, buy one instead, steam the beet until tender and the tops four minutes and serve together. Or better yet, grate the raw beets, chop the tops and toss both in a salad. Remember that it takes less raw food to make a helping than cooked food because nothing is destroyed.

Corn silk, radish, turnip and onion tops can be treated the same way. Carrot tops are good chopped finely and used exactly like parsley, for flavoring and garnish. Any extra of these tops should all be hung for drying in a warm, ventilated room or shelter (attic, porch, shed, etc.) or spread thinly on drying racks. (Never dry herbs in the sun.) Grind and serve them for a vegetable powder. Use as a seasoning or put in gelatin capsules to take as vitamin-mineral supplements. These will be more effective than synthetic vitamins and unchelated minerals.

Do not scrape or peel potatoes, Jerusalem artichokes, carrots, beets, turnips, yams, sweet potatoes and so on. You waste the most nutritious part. Ten percent of the weight of beets, turnips and potatoes is wasted when peeled and three percent of a carrot when scraped. That's like throwing away between three and ten cents of every root vegetable dollar, plus contributing to illnesses through nutritional deficiency.

An elderly neighbor told us of an incident during the depression that illustrated the deficiency aspect of peeling vegetables. She, her husband and six children were living in Kelso, Washington, a town that was singularly depressed the last half of the 1930's. For several years, they lived on weeds and a chicken feed of cracked grains which she slow-cooked. All six children remained strong and healthy. A neighbor family a mile or so back in the woods lived on potatoes. One day the eight-year-old girl of that family came to say her parents, brothers and sister were all dead. When the authorities investigated and learned that the destitute family had been living on potatoes, they wondered why the bright-eyed, active little girl hadn't died as well. On questioning her, they learned that her job, as the youngest sibling, was to carry the potato peelings out to the garbage heap. As she did so after each meal, she munched on the crisp, washed peelings. The vitamins, minerals and enzymes of those raw peelings had kept her healthy and strong. Without them her family had sickened and died.

Every area and climate has edible wild plants, some places literally dozens. New England claims more than 150, the Southland nearly as many. The Pacific Northwest has well over a hundred, and even the Great Plains and the Southwest semi-arid regions and deserts have dozens and dozens. We list a few for starters. For positive knowledge of them and any others that may grow in your area, here is a list of identifiers which can help you:

Local herbalists.

Science and botany professors and teachers of colleges and high schools.

Old timers in your area.

Elderly, local Indians.

Extension Service personnel (state, county).

Agricultural College experimental stations.

Farm people, especially the grandparents.

Local ecologists and survival experts.

When gathering wild edibles, it is a temptation to take too many for immediate use. if you do gather a surplus, wash, dry and hang or spread for dehydrating and store in labeled jars.

Braken: (Brake fern, Wa-ra-be — *Pteris Aquilana-L*)
  Habitat: Damp woods

Edible parts: Fiddlehead sprout or top
Gathering time: Spring, early summer. The tops are good when stem is up to 12 inches high. Snap off two or three inches below curled top. Soak 24 hours in fresh water to which has been added wood ashes (one tablespoon ashes per one gallon water). Wash, chop and add to tossed salad. The taste is nut-like and crisp. Or soak half an hour in hot water, then steam for soup, vegetable dish, or cool and toss in a salad.

Burdock: (Beggar's Button, Burrs — *Articum Lappa-L*)
Habitat: In waste areas everywhere
Edible parts: Young leaves, roots and stems
Gathering time: Spring, early summer. The first year of growth of this biennial is close to the ground. Use tender young leaves for salad, the roots for salad or steamed as a vegetable. Roots in fall are blood and kidney purifiers. Stems of the second-year plants which grow four to five feet are best peeled then steamed and served as asparagus. Burdock is higher in minerals than beets, carrots, potatoes or turnips.

Cattails: (Swamp Bulrush, Cossack Asparagus — *Typha Latifolia-L*)
Habitat: Swamplands and swamps in all climates of the Northern
    Hemisphere
Edible parts: Young shoots and flowerheads or spikes, root stalks
    and stem of lower leaf.
Gathering time: The young shoots are harvested in early spring, and the down from the flowers when they mature. Lower leaf stems are ready in late summer and root stalks in autumn. Young shoots, cut a foot from the root and peeled, are good cooked as an asparagus-type vegetable, or raw in salads. The pollen heads, or down, mixed half-and-half with whole wheat flower, make a delicious bread rich in carbohydrates, protein, sugar, oil and minerals, especially phosphorus. In the fall, harvest the matted, bulbous roots. They are high in starch and sugar. Wash, dry and grind to a sweet flour similar to rice or corn flour. It makes excellent pancakes, cookies and muffins.

Chickweed: *(Stellaria Media)*
Habitat: Waste areas and gardens
Edible parts: Leaves
Gathering time: Spring to fall. Protected with a leaf mulch, it can be gathered through the winter in moderate climates. Use the leaves raw in salads. They are rich in iron.

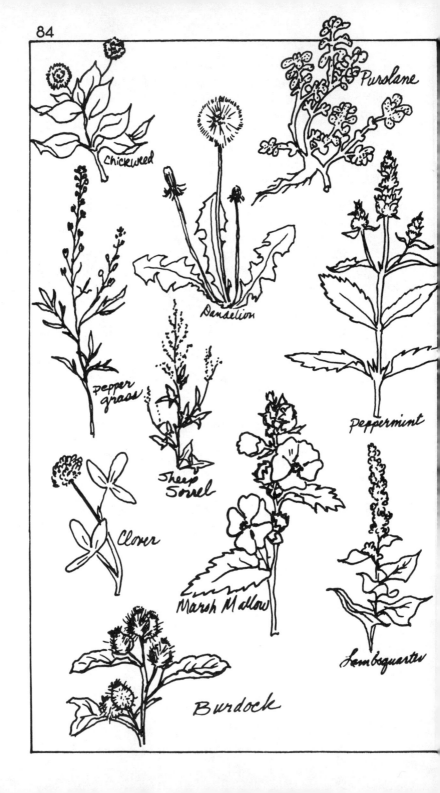

Chickweed

Purslane

Dandelion

Pepper grass

Peppermint

Sheep Sorrel

Clover

Marsh Mallow

Lambsquarter

Burdock

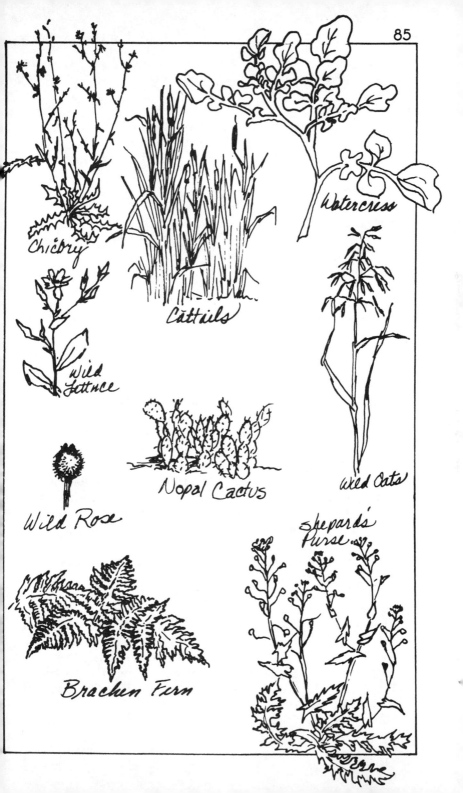

Chicory

Watercress

Cattails

Wild Lettuce

Nopal Cactus

Wild Oats

Wild Rose

shepard's Purse

Bracken Fern

Chicory: (Blue Sailors or Wild Endive — *Chickorium Intybus-L)*
Habitat: Roadsides, waste areas, sandy soil
Edible parts: Young leaves, roots
Gathering time: Leaves in early spring, roots in early summer.
Slice roots lengthwise and dehydrate well (they mold easily).
Roots may be chopped for adding to a salad or steamed to serve as
a warm vegetable. Leaves are used as a salad. Dried roots may be
roasted and used as a substitute for coffee. Chicory contains no
harmful stimulating caffeine.

Clover (Red): *(Trifolium Pratense-L)*
Habitat: Fields, wastelands, roadsides of temperate climates
Edible parts: Young leaves, prime blossoms
Gathering time: Spring for leaves, summer for blossoms. The
leaves are used as lettuce for salads, tacos, sandwiches and in
coleslaw. Blossoms should be picked when near or in full bloom
and immediately eaten in a salad or dried for making tea.

Dandelion: *(Taraxacum Oficinale)*
Habitat: Grasslands, gardens, roadsides, fields in all climates
Edible parts: Roots, leaves, buds, flowers, stems
Gathering time: Early spring for leaves, late spring, early fall for
flowers and buds, all seasons for roots. The leaves are good
chopped and added to salads or steamed, seasoned with onion,
vinegar, lemon or other herbs and served as spinach. Buds are
excellent, nut-like morsels in salads and for a tea for tonic and
indigestion. Young roots are good chopped and added to salads, or
ground and used as a caffeine-free coffee substitute, when dark-
roasted. Dandelion leaves are many times richer in Vitamin A,
potassium and calcium than leaf lettuce or even spinach.

Lambsquarter: (Wild Spinach, Goosefoot — *Chenopadium*
                   Album-L)
Habitat: Gardens, cultivated fields in most all climates
Edible Parts: Tender leaves and stems
Gathering time: Early spring to fall after late summer cultivation
and rains. The first tender shoots from four to six inches tall or
tender leaves of taller plants should be used in salads. Later when
plants are larger, the leaves and immature fruits may be steamed
and served as spinach. As is the case for all wild edibles, surplus
leaves and fruits should be dehydrated and stored for winter
seasonings, soups and loaves, both bread and nut-meat ones.

Mallow: (Malva, Cheese Plant, Low Mallow — *Malva Rotundifolia*)
Habitat: Gardens, rich cultivated fields
Edible parts: Leaves
Gathering time: Summer. The leaves are used in salads, Mallow, or Malva as the plant is commonly called, contains all the healing substances of asparagin, pectin and mucilage, all especially restorative for the respiratory, alimentary and urinary organs. Centuries ago, Pliny wrote of the wonders of Low Mallow to the effect that whoever ate a spoonful of it every day would be free of diseases.

Other related species having many uses for hundreds of years are hollyhock, okra, high mallow and marsh mallow.

Nopal Cactus: (Giant Prickly Pear — *Opuntia*)
Habitat: Southwest desert, semi-arid lands, and Mexico
Edible parts: Leaves, fruits
Gathering time: All year round for leaves, after flowers bloom and fall off in late spring for fruit. Cut off large leaves five to eight inches long, whittle off prickles and spear needles, wash, chop and add to salads. Or serve in long sticks, like carrot sticks. Nopal is marvelously rich in all minerals, vitamins and protein. It has a mild taste and can be used to make boiled gumbo vegetable soups. The fruits can be eaten raw (very tart) or with honey or fructose added, made into jelly or cactus candy.

Peppergrass: (Cress, Land Cress, Bird's Pepper — *Lapidium Virginicum*)
Habitat: Sandy, dry soil, temperate to hot climates
Edible parts: Leaves and seeds
Gathering time: Leaves in spring and early summer, seeds after flowering when seed pods are still green. Peppergrass leaves and seeds should not be cooked. Try to gather plenty to dry and store. They keep for two years. The spicy, pungent flavor greatly enhances finished soups, coleslaw and salads, green drinks, seed or nut-meat loaves and pizza.

Peppermint: (Brandy Mint, American Mint, Lamb Mint — *Mentha Piperita-L*)
Habitat: Damp places in primitive areas, wet, low places, along sides of streams, marshlands
Edible parts: Leaves and flowers
Gathering time: Spring, summer, fall. Cut flowering end before flowers mature. Fresh green leaves can be used in both vegetable and fruit salads, in fruit drinks, in jellies and sauces. Dried leaves

and flowers make an excellent, soothing, healthful (especially to nerves and digestion) and a most relaxing beverage for all of us in a tense, overactive age. The flavor of mint is used more than any other, and universally liked.

Spearmint is a relative of peppermint but not quite as versatile, popular or beneficial as peppermint (which is even good for babies).

Purslane: (Pussley, Portulaca — *Portulaca Oleracea*)
Habitat: Fertile garden soil, warm to temperate climates
Cultivated in Europe and Mexico and sold in Mexican markets
Edible parts: Leaves
Gathering time: All during the growing season. Use in salads or steamed as spinach. Eat every day and dry the surplus. It is richer in vitamins and minerals than garden vegetables.

Sheep Sorrel: (Sour Grass, Little Vinegar — *Rumex Acetosella-L*)
Habitat: Waste areas of sandy soil in most climates
Edible parts: Leaves
Gathering time: Late summer and early fall. This tart-tasting salad flavorer, high in potassium, tartaric acid and Vitamin C, should be eaten all season and surpluses dried and powdered for off-season uses. It is especially good for fevers and colds.

Shepherd's Purse: (Lady's Purse, Pepper and Salt —
Capsella Bursa-pastoris-L)
Habitat: Waste areas, sandy, gravelly soil
Edible parts: Fruits, leaves
Gathering time: The leaves should be gathered in early spring before the plant flowers, the fruit before it matures completely. Shepherd's Purse is so extremely rich in Vitamins A and C and so valuable as a diuretic (among other properties), that it should be gathered faithfully by all. The peppery taste adds much to foods. When seeds are mature, gather along with leaves for drying and storing to perk up winter soups, salads and protein dishes.

Watercress: *(Nasturtium Officinale)*
Habitat: Slow moving, gravelly streams
Edible parts: Leaves
Gathering time: Spring to early summer. If the bottom of the stream is muddy, do not gather. Several cuttings of watercress can be made a season. No wild edible has enjoyed a longer and more accepted spot in history, from the ancient Middle East to Old England. Not only is it rich in Vitamins C and A, B, E and G, it

contains a notable amount of potassium, sodium, calcium, magnesium, iron, manganese, copper and sulfur. Never cook watercress. Add it to completed dishes and use it daily if possible.

Wild Lettuce: (Prickly Lettuce — *Lactuca Scariola-L*)
Habitat: Rich soil of primitive areas in mild and temperate climates
Edible parts: First tender shoots, leaves
Gathering time: Early spring when four to six inches high. Wild lettuce, a forerunner of the cultivated varieties, is eaten raw in salads. Most animals eat it voraciously.

Wild Oats: *(Uvularia Perfoliata)*
Habitat: Open fields, pasturelands, roadsides in most climates
Edible parts: Young shoots
Gathering time: Spring. The young plants are good steamed and served as one would asparagus shoots.

Wild Rose: (Brier Rose, Dog Rose — *Rosa Canina-L*)
Habitat: Waste areas, roadsides, rocky soil
Edible parts: Petals, leaves, fruit (hips, red or orange)
Gathering time: Midsummer for petals and leaves, late summer to early fall for ripe hips. Fresh rose petals and leaves tossed in a fruit or vegetable salad and/or sprinkled on top provide elegance as well as extra nutrition. Dry petals for tea. Ripe rose hips are marvelously rich in Vitamin C, each hip containing ten milligrams. They also contain a high amount of carotene (Vitamin A precursor) and Vitamin P (bioflavonoids). Rose hips can be used for tea or the syrupy pulp, when squeezed out through a colander or cheese cloth and ground with water added, can be used for sauce or drink. (Sweeten with one teaspoon of honey per glass or helping.)

Traveling And Eating Out

"A healthy body is the guest chamber of the soul; a sick one its prison."

Francis Bacon

A common question put to an all-raw food devotee is, "Do you ever eat out?" When the answer is *yes,* another question immediately follows. "What can you find to eat?"

Ten years ago the answer was greatly involved. Today it is comparatively simple. There are salad bars in many restaurants, with more and more turning to this sensible, appetizing and nutritious way to please their clientele and keep them coming back. More and more people each year are avoiding highly processed foods, especially when they entertain guests.

It's a poor restaurant today that fails to serve a salad, skimpy as it may be. However, many "good" restaurants will serve only a small salad containing little more than the nearly worthless iceberg lettuce.

In our pockets or purse, we always carry a small cellophane bag of mixed sprouts or sprouted seeds, or a generous slice of seed cheese. When we quietly explain to waiters that we are raw-food vegetarians, they give us an understanding nod as we order a large salad with lemon on the side.

It is not unusual to find a restaurant that serves a menu of vegetables. If they are slightly boiled or steam cooked and there is an accompanying salad, we occasionally order it. However, we do not order if it is a stir-fry vegetable plate. The cooked fats are too indigestible.

Some restaurants serve raw fruits, either whole or in a salad, in which case we have no problem. One should remember, when ordering, to check on the dressing. Too often, for many of us, that dressing has a yogurt base. We are delighted to report, however, that the use of tahini dressing (sesame seed butter) flavored with cinnamon is catching on. Of course, tahini is made with oil but if you have a good digestion you can probably take a little now and then. One can always order fresh fruit salad or fruit plate without dressing.

When Elizabeth was struggling for survival and on a mono-diet, we carried fruit (ungassed bananas, unsprayed apples or pears, fresh fruit in season or cantaloupe) in a neatly closed paper bag and explained our problem of eating privately to the maitre d'hotel. By approaching him before diners began to arrive, or after the rush hours, we found him on each occasion to be most gracious. He took the paper bag, seated us, then saw to it that when our order was served, there was the fruit, ready to eat, attractively peeled and displayed. Such service, of course, deserves a generous tip to maitre d' and waiter. Those occasions were pleasant and special.

The raw food or limited diet way of eating is not a problem when traveling if a few plans and preparations are made in advance. With the exception of Russia and a few remote parts of the world, most countries have an abundance of fresh fruits and vegetables to offer the tourist in summer. Hotels in the European and Scandinavian countries, Central and South American countries, Canada, New Zealand, Australia and many African countries offer salads of local fresh fruits and vegetables. In our experience, tropical countries offer the most raw fare, especially fruits. In Mexico, Central and South America, hotels always feature fresh fruit.

Nevertheless, in traveling, we take some concentrated foods in a small bag or carryall, namely seeds for sprouting, dried fruits and freshly shelled almonds which keep unrefrigerated longer than most shelled nuts. On the average, we eat about half of our meals in our hotel room or on a picnic outing.

For instance, on a recent three-week trip to Mexico we took the following from home:

½ cup alfalfa seeds (makes 8 one-pint bags of sprouts.) $ .79
1 cup adzuki beans (makes 6 one-pint bags of 3-day
  sprouts, more when in tropical climes,
  less in cool altitude.)   .29
1 cup sesame seeds (makes 6 to 9 one-pint bags
  of sprouts.)   .38
2 cups sunflower seeds (seeds double in size when
  sprouted 12 to 24 hours. We soak 1/3 cup at a time.)   .66
1½ cups almonds   2.03
1 lb. dates   1.89
1 lb. figs   2.09
1 lb. raisins   1.85
1 lb. dried apples (home grown, dried)   .00

The total weight is 6 pounds. This amount of food cost us a total of $9.98.

The food from home was 30% of the food we ate on the trip. We bought another 30% at markets and 40% in restaurants. Here is the breakdown of our food costs for the 21-day trip.

Food brought from home	$ 9.98
Fresh victuals in markets	28.75
Meals in restaurants	227.80

Since salad meals are less costly than conventional ones, our restaurant bills are much less than those of the average tourist. Our total food bill while traveling is far less than most travelers, and we never stray far from our raw-food regimen.

For seed sprouting we use hotel-provided drinking glasses topped with nylon net held on by rubber bands. Or we use plastic freezing bags we bring from home. We soak seeds in the plastic bags overnight. In the morning we make holes in them with a large safety pin, drain, wash then drain again. We use plastic hook clothes pins for holding the bags and hang the hooks over the shower rod or faucets for good draining between rinses. With two shallow plastic soup plates, knives, forks and spoons, a cutting knife and paper towels for hand towels and napkins, we manage conveniently and with a minimum of bother, weight and cost. We also travel with two hard plastic glasses and a quart bottle of hard plastic for water to take on outings, to the beach, on picnics or on short boat trips.

Water has been and still is a matter of major concern while traveling. Most cities of the world, and even towns, chlorinate their drinking water to kill organisms. However, chlorine is itself very harmful. It destroys many of the vitamins we ingest or synthesize in our bodies. Fortunately there is a way to largely overcome this problem if the management of the hotel you choose does not provide pure water — mineral, filtered or distilled.

On arriving in your hotel room and discovering you are dependent on tap water, fill the provided bathroom glasses with hot water. As the water cools, the chlorine escapes and you will find that after a few hours, very little chlorine remains.

A word about eating raw foods in foreign countries. We've known many people who've traveled weeks and months at a time without ever eating any fresh salads or fruits for fear of getting travelers' diarrhea. Yet many suffer from that joy-stealer anyway, invariably blaming the food or lack of cleanliness.

Actually, the blame usually falls back on the eater for a combination of reasons. In spite of tourists thinking they are relaxed because they're on vacation, they too often are excited with all the planned activities and the sights, frequently hurrying, grabbing a bite so they can do this, go there, see that. As a result, they eat hurriedly and often too much, overloading the digestive system and overtaxing the strength.

Most people in the United States live at little above sea level. When they go to Mexico City or the Alps of Europe or the high climes of South America or Asia, they may have 20% to 40% less oxygen than they're accustomed to at home. They may be breathing air that has up to 35% less oxygen and their bodies (lung capacity, blood count, etc.) are not adjusted to it.

When food is taken into the body, some 25% of the blood supply goes to the stomach to help digest the food. If the person unaccustomed to altitude continues to walk or climb stairs or carry on physical activity, he may experience one of two things. Either he becomes fatigued and is forced to rest, or his digestion rebels, in which case it gets rid of the burden quickly by vomiting or diarrhea. With the digestive sickness, the traveler is sure he has a case of the parasitic *turista* or has eaten bad food.

In high altitudes, one should eat lightly, drink sparingly of alcohol or none at all, and rest fifteen minutes to a half hour after each meal.

Occasionally, someone will get bad bacteria or amoeba. In all our experience of traveling and living in foreign countries, we have had such trouble only once. That was many years ago before we learned that if we have sufficient hydrochloric acid in our stomachs, we have no problem with bacteria and parasites. They cannot survive the strong acid environment of a healthy stomach. If we chew food enough, we activate the production of saliva, and the saliva swallowed with the food stimulates the production of hydrochloric acid in the stomach.

Americans are fast eaters. They do not chew their food well. Most of them over the age of 40, and many under it (even children), have a deficiency of hydrochloric acid. Today, many doctors, finally recognizing the problem, advise their patients to buy glutamic acid hydrochloride tablets at health food stores before they leave on a trip and take from one to three tablets with each meal. This not only provides protection from bad organisms, but helps food to digest as well.

For most travelers who experience motion sickness (sea sickness, plane or car sickness), there is a remedy. This distress is usually helped or eliminated by taking B vitamins with extra B_6

before and during the trip. Although some feel that powdered brewer's yeast, high in the B vitamins, is too concentrated a food, we recommend it over synthetic vitamin pills. It is easy to take and easily digested.

For at least two weeks before your trip, take primary brewer's yeast grown on molasses. Torula nutritional yeast is cheaper but does not agree with some people. It is cultured on wood pulp and has a strange taste. Red Star is a good bulk brand that is not expensive.

Start by taking a one-half teaspoonful of yeast three times a day in water, juice or foods at mealtime. Increase a bit each time you take it until you are taking a tablespoonful with each meal. If you suffer frequently from motion sickness, you may want to take natural-source vitamin B_6 tablets in addition to the yeast.

Travel light and enjoy your trip.

When invited to the home of friends or family, express your joy in the invitation and accept it. Then quietly, briefly mention your food program to the hostess, at the same time letting her know there is no problem. Tell her you eat very simply and ask her to allow you to supplement your plate with a food or two that carries and serves easily. Find out what vegetable and/or salad she plans to serve, or what fruit, and tell her what you can bring. If she offers to fix what you want, for her convenience, ask what she has on hand. Then make your selection and make it simple.

When dinner time arrives, do not call attention to your serving but accept with calm and a sense of humor if attention focuses on it. That will soon pass, conversation will turn to other interesting and curious things, and the meal will proceed as though you are eating everything everyone else is.

We have gone to only a few dinner parties under such circumstances (Elizabeth cannot break from the diet) where the hostess has simplified the menu and found to her joy that the guests still loved it. Sometimes the menu is improved for having been simplified, and it is enjoyed because of more fresh foods and fewer rich and processed ones being served.

When we entertain, we choose raw foods that people generally like and only occasionally do we make a concession to conventional cookery by serving baked whole grain muffins or trout-rice casserole or baked salmon. We have yet to find a person who hasn't eaten heartily of our party fare.

Brown-Bagging For Lunch

*"Build yourselves houses and dwell in them;
plant gardens and eat the fruit thereof."*
                                                    Jeremiah 29:5

How well we remember the wail that Elizabeth let out when, after deciding on an all-raw nutritional program, we were faced with having to prepare lunches to carry to the office! No baked breads, no crackers, chips or even the innocent tortilla to wrap around a taco stuffing.

There was our answer: a Romaine "tortilla" made into a taco. We were on our way. From that tiny beginning has come a host of brown bag and lunch box meals we thoroughly enjoy and anticipate.

Here are a few to show you some possibilities. You'll be able to put together countless different nutritional and delightful lunches. These lunches are designed for one person.

Taco Lunch 1 large Romaine leaf wrapped around the following: ¼ mashed avocado, with ¼ cup sunflower seed sprouts, ¼ teaspoon kelp. Yam sticks for dessert.

Banana Lunch 3 or 4 bananas, 2 slices raisin sprouted oat bread, with or without fruit spread.

Apple Pecan Lunch 2 or 3 apples, 8 to 12 pecans, depending on your height, bone structure and physical activity.

Celery Lunch 6 sticks celery stuffed with soy cheese and 2 slices Essene bread.

Lettuce Sandwich Lunch Romaine or butter lettuce leaves spread with sesame blue cheese and topped by other leaves, and carrot sticks.

Cheese and Cracker Lunch 2 or 3 slices of flaxseed cheese, several wheat crackers and a small plastic bag of sunflower lettuce (eat with fingers).

Bible Times Lunch Fresh figs and grapes, or dried figs and raisins. (Figs are a complete food, providing adequate protein.)

Artichoke Lunch Slices of Jerusalem artichoke (unpeeled) spread with sunflower seed cheese, served with ripe olives and fresh radishes.

When brown bagging, try the mono-diet. Here is a list of foods we frequently eat singly, with excellent, sustained energy resulting. We eat no more than a pound, less if the food is more concentrated, as bananas or persimmons.

Bananas   Apples
Grapes   Persimmons
Figs (16 to 20)   Pears
Cabbage (½ head)   Fresh Prunes
Jerusalem artichokes   Cherrries
Carrots   Jicama

As you become accustomed to a raw-food brown-bag lunch, you will invent many more menus, and try more single foods. We find we enjoy making a meal on any one of the Essene or Essene-type breads. Sometimes we use a fruit spread to make the lunch even more special.

Recipes For The Diet Of The Future

"Living food, living health; dead food, dying health."

Anonymous

Food preparation is one of the oldest rituals of civilized man. Not only is the quality of foods of utmost importance — freshness, color, texture, aroma — but also the utensils they are prepared with and served in. From gourds, hollowed wood and sea shells to earthenware, refined ceramics and metals, these utensils have always been and are now prized household possessions and clearly reflect the culture of the time and place.

This is still true today despite mass production and world trade. As in every age, however, some utensils today are better than others. Although hard plastic bowls, dishpans, or vegetable wash-pans may be used, we recommend stainless steel, enamel and glass ones which can also be used for soaking, mixing and storing. Cooking should be done in stainless steel, glass, cast iron or Corningware and similar types. Aluminum, a fairly soft metal, is not recommended, especially for cooking. Small amounts of aluminum are dissolved from the pan by the foods, especially acids and high protein foods. Nor are the stickless, coated types of cooking utensils recommended. Although recently improved, they are still made from petroleum products and gas off. Soft plastic for food serving and storage — covered bowls, boxes, bottles, jars, etc. — are to be avoided. They also are made from petroleum products. Most people are sensitive to them and some are ill because of eating foods stored and served in them. Some types of earthen and enamelware containing lead, a toxic metal, should be avoided. Most of these types have gone off the market in the United States but at this writing, some are still being made in Mexico.

Nothing has as yet been found better than glass, china and all such related ware as crockery and stoneware for cooking, baking and table service. Naturally finished (oiled) wooden serving pieces are also excellent for salad and fruit service, an interesting part of your table setting.

With preparation, cooking and table service at your disposal and your fresh, living foods in your kitchen, you are ready to consider the recipes that follow. But before you do, you will want to consider seasonings.

Remember that food seasoning began as a method of preserving foods hundreds of years before refrigeration was generally available. Salt was one of the first preservatives used. Several hundred years ago salt peter (potassium nitrate or sodium nitrate) was found to preserve meats (ham, bacon, sausage), and nearly three hundred years ago refined table sugar was discovered to be an effective preservative.

These old customs have remained with us to this day, ruining some of the nutrition in our foods, addicting us to their use and destroying our health.

In the nutrition of the future, they will all be left out — the hot, burning peppers, the overstimulating condiments, the highly flavorful foods that contain small amounts of a toxic element as does laurel, all of the lily family — onion, garlic, shallot, chive, leek, etc. — and such bitter herbs as golden seal and tranquilizing teas like catnip.

You'll notice that the addition of onion in the recipes that follow is optional. If your liver is functioning well and can detoxify the allynin in the onion family, by all means use them on the transitional diet. As you get farther and farther into the program, eating mostly raw foods, your taste will become more acute and you will depend less and less on strong flavors, spices and condiments.

Salt is no doubt the most difficult seasoning to give up. Salt is optional in the recipes that follow. Sodium (salt) is an essential mineral in the body. Since sodium occurs naturally in foods, its supply is sufficient for most of us. However, in some areas of heavier rainfall, sodium may be leached out of the soil. In that case, a small amount of sea salt might be used, or better, kelp, dulse and sea plants.

The current fashion is to condemn salt as a nonfood, yet it is an essential nutrient just as calcium or magnesium or potassium is. The reason that table salt, or even the more acceptable sea salt, may be harmful is that it is not in a chelated form, as it is in nature.

Chelated, in simple terms, means *grabbed onto.* In the seaplant *kelp,* for instance, salt is grabbed onto and carried along the digestive tract with many other trace nutrients that enable it to be absorbed slowly, efficiently, as nature intended, and not all in the *naked dose* we get when we put (concentrated) table salt on our food and so overtax our system.

The recipes for entrees that follow—the salads, vegetable dishes, protein loaves, balls, patties, sauces and beverages—are flexible. You can change them to suit your taste or your supply of foods on hand. We suggest, however, you make the breads, cookies, desserts, cheeses, yogurts and bread foods according to recipes and suggestions until you are familiar with them. Then you can vary, invent, create and improvise on the recipes to your heart's content.

You will need at least a food chopper-grinder with graded discs or parts for coarse and fine grinding. A blender is very helpful but not absolutely necessary. A seed-nut mill is advisable. However, a very fine disc on some grinders does an acceptable job of meal-making. It might be necessary to grind a second time. You will find the Chop-rite hand grinder or the Wheatena (which is the Chop-rite converted to an electric grinder), excellent for not only grinding wheat grass, but sprouted grains as well. An attachment will grind seeds to meals.

ENTREES

SEED MEAT CASSEROLE

1 cup 12 to 30 hour
  sprouted sunflower seeds
1 pinch of salt (optional)
1 teaspoon butter or oil

Mix in a stainless steel bowl set in a larger pan of warm water no more than 110° Farenheit. (You can barely endure your finger in it for testing.) Cover, set aside in a warm place for 10 minutes. Serve in preheated custard cups. (This simple recipe is an all-time favorite.) Serves 2 to 4.

BRAZIL NUT LOUIE

2 leaves of Romaine or bib
  lettuce

1 cup shredded lettuce

½ cup grated cucumber (or
  carrot, parsnip, turnip)

1 avocado

1 teaspoon kelp

¼ cup coarsely chopped
  Brazil nuts

1 tablespoon chopped parsley or onion (optional)

1 large tomato

Place the chopped lettuce on the Romaine or lettuce leaf. Peal and mash avocado and add grated vegetable, parsley or onion, kelp and Brazils. Spoon onto the lettuce in a mound and top with parsley sprig. Cut the tomato in ¾ inch wedges and arrange around the nut louie mound. Serves 2 to 4.

NUT-MEAT LOAF

1½ cups of sesame seed meal

1 cup ground carrots or
  carrot pulp

1 cup ground celery

¼ cup chopped, reconsti-
  tuted dulse

½ cup chopped filberts, (or
  other nuts)

1 tablespoon flaxseed meal

½ teaspoon dried onion
  (optional)

½ teaspoon paprika
  (optional)

water of fermec for stiff
  dough

Mix together, adding water last. Press into oiled custard cups to mold. Set aside until they have reached room temperature. Unmold on dinner plates or platter. Garnish with thin carrot circles or a sprig of celery leaves. Serves 4 to 6.

THANKSGIVING TURKEY FANTASY

1 cup almond meal

2 cups ground celery and juice

1 tomato

⅛ teaspoon sage (optional)

½ teaspoon dry parsley or 1 tablespoon fresh, chopped parsley

½ teaspoon kelp powder

1 tablespoon flaxseed meal

Peel and mash tomato. Mix well all ingredients. Mixture should be stiff. If not, add a little more almond or flaxseed meal. Press into a well oiled, turkey-shaped cookie cutter and unmold on shredded lettuce on colored plates. Garnish with carrot slices cut in the shape of wings and serve with cranberry sauce. Makes 4 "turkeys".

SEED MEAT PIE

½ cup pumpkin seeds

½ cup flaxseed meal

2 cups grated zucchini, jicama, potato or Jerusalem artichoke

1 cup finely chopped lettuce

½ cup sprouted seed, finely chopped (any kind can be used but we like sunflower best)

½ teaspoon salt (optional) or 1 teaspoon kelp

¼ cup reconstituted dulse, chopped fermec or soak water or dulse water

1 tablespoon chopped celery

Mix all together, adding enough water to make a medium stiff dough. Line an oiled pie pan with pie crust (see recipe) then smooth the nut-meat pie filling over it. Sprinkle with sesame seeds and set aside to reach room temperature, allowing flavors to blend and pie to firm up. Serve cold or warm. (In oven 10 minutes at 100°.) Garnish with thin circles of carrots or radishes stuck edgewise in the filling. Cut in wedges. Serves 6.

GARDEN NUT-MEAT BALLS

1 cup chopped pecans

½ cup flaxseed meal

½ cup ground cauliflower

1 cup alfalfa sprouts, chopped

12 sprouted garbanzos, marinated in oil (optional) and lemon juice a few hours and chopped

1 cup ground celery and its juice

2 tablespoons chopped green nasturtium seeds or watercress or radish

2 teaspoons kelp

1 teaspoon chopped onion or ¼ teaspoon onion powder (optional)

Mix all together and knead. Set aside for an hour. If the mixture is not a stiff dough, add a little more flaxseed meal, soy flour or rice flour. Make into meat balls the size of walnuts. Serve with tomato or mushroom sauce, cold or warm. Serves 6.

SEED MEAT PATTIES

1 cup pumpkin seed or sunflower seeds, sprouted

1 cup ground comfrey root (any root vegetable may be substituted)

1 teaspoon celery seed

1 teaspoon onion or 1 clove of garlic (optional)

¼ cup parsley or radish tops

1 hot chili pepper (optional)

½ cup of 24-hour sprouted wheat, barley, oats or rye

Grind ingredients, one after the other, and mix thoroughly. If necessary, add a little water to make into a workable dough. Set mixing bowl in hot, not boiling, water for an hour for flavors to blend and dough to adhere. Form into ½ inch thick patties. Serve on hot plates with favorite warm sauce. Serves 6 to 8.

POTATO-SEED CASSEROLE

1 whole, large, grated
   potato
½ cup sprouted flaxseed,
   ground
1 large tomato, diced
1 teaspoon kelp

Mix and serve in mounds on lettuce leaf. (Other seasonings may be added.) Serves 2 to 4.

ROLLED TACOS

½ cup finely ground nuts
¼ cup flaxseed meal or chia
   meal
3 to 4 tablespoons fresh
   tomato, juice and pulp
   (we mash a medium
   tomato)
1 chili pepper, finely
   chopped or ground, or
   dash of cayenne
1 teaspoon chopped onion
   (optional)
¼ teaspoon salt (optional)
   or 1 teaspoon kelp
1 cup alfalfa sprouts
6 tortillas

Mix all except sprouts together to make a rather stiff paste. Measure a heaping tablespoon onto each tortilla, sprinkle with sprouts, make into a roll and serve with or without a sauce. Makes 6 tortillas. Serves 2 to 4.

ENCHILADAS

6 to 8 tortillas

   Almond Butter (or any
   nut butter or sunflower
   seed cheese or raw peanut
   butter), thinned with a
   little oil

   Lettuce, finely shredded

   Tomato slices (and/or
   onion and bell pepper
   rings)

   Mashed avocado, thinned
   with water to consistency
   of cream

   Diced radish

   Salt and pepper to taste
   (optional)

Place the tortillas on a large platter or tray. Spread almond butter on tortillas. Add remaining ingredients in order listed.

BREADS and PASTRY

Many times, a raw-food vegetarian will have a continuing craving or need for more carbohydrates and protein. The following recipes for breads, crackers and so on, meet that need and fit beautifully in the unfired food regimen.

Raw grains should rarely be eaten. In them, a substance called phytate, phytic acid or phytin, ties up zinc in the body and can cause a deficiency of this vital trace mineral utilized in so many bodily functions.

Cooking the grains inactivates much of the phytate, but the cooked starch and cooked protein of bread is difficult for the system to digest. Allergists conservatively estimate that 65% of the population in the United States is allergic to wheat and 45% is allergic to corn. By contrast, few people are allergic to sprouted cereal grains of any kind.

Phytin is inactivated in the sprouting process within the cereal grain seeds. The seed starch is mostly converted to simple sugars (fructose) which is much easier to digest. Proteins convert to amino acids, a process the stomach has to do when proteins are ingested. This protein conversion makes them essentially predigested. These amino acids (predigested proteins) and simple sugars (converted starch) are readily assimilated by the digestive system. They are excellent high energy foods and easily digested.

Because the fermenting action in these breads is still present, they should be refrigerated and eaten within three days. We often slice the bread, wrap separately and freeze for later serving. Take them out and thaw for 20-30 minutes before warming and eating.

Before making raw and Essene type breads, spread the sprouted grains on a tray or cookie sheet for an hour prior to grinding. This dries off the excess moisture without drying out the sprouted grain. The bread will be firmer and tastier. (Excess moisture makes a watery, doughy bread.)

RYE BREAD

2 cups whole grain rye, sprouted and fine ground twice

¼ cup reconstituted, chopped dulse (optional)

½ cup chopped, sprouted sunflower seed or nuts (optional)

1 tablespoon caraway seed

½ teaspoon salt (optional)

Mix all together. Knead well and form into log. Set aside, covered with cloth, 8 to 12 hours for flavors to blend. Wrap in plastic wrap or cellophane. Store in the refrigerator. It keeps up to ten days. This bread is delicious served warm. We lay slices of it on a grate over a low burner to warm but not toast.

CORN BREAD

2 cups of sprouted corn, ground

¼ cup golden (brown can be used) flaxseed meal

½ cup finely chopped nuts or 12-hour sunflower seed sprouts

1 tablespoon oil or melted butter (for taste we prefer the butter)

1 teaspoon kelp

¼ teaspoon salt (optional)

Mix all together and knead, adding a little water if too dry for binding. Set aside for 1 to 2 hours. Roll in wax paper and refrigerate. Slice thin for serving. It may be warmed to 100° and served on preheated plates.

BARLEY BREAD

2 cups sprouted barley,
  finely ground (1¼ cups
  dry barley makes 2 cups
  sprouted)
½ cup ground dried figs
1 teaspoon kelp

Grind all together and knead.
Form into loaf or roll and set
aside for 12 hours before serving. Wrap in wax paper to
refrigerate. Slice for serving.

RAISIN CARROT BREAD

2 cups sprouted buck-
  wheat, ground
1 cup grated carrots (or
  carrot pulp from juicing)
¼ cup flaxseed meal
½ cup chopped filberts
¼ cup ground raisins
1 tablespoon honey
1 teaspoon kelp or 2 tablespoons reconstituted
  dulse

Mix and knead to a stiff
dough, adding water only if
necessary. Form into a loaf or
log. Set aside until serving
time to allow the bread to season and bind for good slicing.
Slices may be warmed and
served on preheated plates.

ESSENE BREAD (Plain)

Wheat berries, whole barley or whole rye were used in the making of Essene bread. Here's how:

1 to 2 cups wheat, barley or rye (or any combination of the three)

½ teaspoon salt (optional) or 2 teaspoons kelp

Soak grain 8-12 hours and leave to sprout 16-48 hours or until sprout is length of the grain. (Rinse and drain 2 or 3 times during sprouting.) Grind the sprouted grains with hand grinder, using fine disc, or in a Champion blender or such grinders as Chop-rite or Wheatena. Grind twice if necessary to make a finely ground mass. Add salt or kelp. Knead until dough binds. Make into 2-inch thick loaves or patties, or large 1-inch thick circles. Place in the sun for several hours, turning now and then, or in a warm place (75° to 90°) until dry on the outside.

ESSENE BREAD VARIATIONS

1. To the Essene bread dough, add 1 to 2 cups of finely chopped vegetables, as celery, parsley, bell pepper, radish or carrot, in any combination or singly.
2. When grinding the sprouted grain, add from 1 to 2 tablespoons of celery seed, caraway, poppy, dill or sesame seed.
3. While grinding the sprouted grain, add ½ cup of figs, dates or raisins.

OATMEAL-RAISIN BREAD

2 cups hulless oats, sprouted 48 to 72 hours

½ cup raisins

2 teaspoons kelp or ½ teaspoon salt

½ cup chopped nuts (optional)

Fine-grind oats and raisins, add kelp and nuts. Mix and knead until dough binds well. Make into log, set in sun for 4 hours or leave uncovered at room temperature overnight. Refrigerate. Slice for serving.

BUCKWHEAT PANCAKES

2 cups sprouted buck-
wheat, ground

½ cup fermec (see page 151)

½ teaspoon sodium bicar-
bonate or potassium
bicarbonate

½ teaspoon salt or 1 tea-
spoon kelp

Mix all together. Drop in spoonfuls on plastic wrap. Place in dehydrator or pre-heated, turned-off oven for 25 minutes. Turn pancakes over on a pan, plastic wrap and all, then peel off plastic wrap and dehydrate another 15 minutes. Serve warm on preheated plates. Soft butter and warm honey or pure maple syrup make an excellent topping.

RAISIN WHEAT BREAD

2 cups sprouted wheat,
ground

½ cup raisins, ground

¼ cup reconstituted,
drained, chopped dulse

Mix together and knead. Make into a loaf or log, set aside a few hours or overnight. Refrigerate. Slice for serving.

OAT BREAD

2 cups sprouted oats

½ cup Brazils, chopped

1 tablespoon dill seed

1 teaspoon salt (optional)

Rice or soy flour, if
necessary, to make a stiff,
adhesive dough

Fine grind oats. Mix all and knead, adding flour only if necessary for a stiff, binding dough. Form into a loaf, place in oiled dish or wax paper, set aside a few hours or over-night. Refrigerate, slice and warm, serving on warm plates.
Note: For a delicious sweet bread to serve with a fruit meal, use ½ cup raisins, dates, figs or dehydrated bananas, chopped or ground, instead of Brazil nuts and dill seed.

VARIATIONS:
RICE BREAD

Rice Bread: Make the same as Oat Bread but use sprouted rice and filberts instead of Brazils

Millet Bread: Make the same as Oat Bread but use sprouted millet, pecans and poppy seeds instead of Brazils and dill seed.

CRACKERS

All crackers can be made without flaxseed meal. However, for a crisper, noncrumbling cracker, add 2 or 3 tablespoons of flaxseed meal and a few teaspoons of water to the dough. We like to flavor crackers with different kinds of seeds. Onion salt may be used also. For more proteins, B vitamins and minerals, add from 1 to 4 tablespoons of brewer's yeast to the recipes for crackers. Crackers can be made in all cut shapes —square, triangLe, etc. —or dropped from a spoon and made into rounds.

WHEAT CRACKERS

2 cups wheat berries
1 teaspoon salt (optional)
   Soak water or plain water
   Sprout wheat berries for 24 hours (yields approx. 4 cups sprouted wheat).

Grind fine, work into a dough, with or without salt, and then add soak water or water to make a very thick cream. (This can be made in a blender.) Cover a large cookie sheet with wax paper, or cellophane and spread dough over all. Dehydrate at 100° in a dehydrator or in preheated, turned-off oven. Mark in squares when half dry. When crisp, break into squares and store in sealed container in a cool, dry place. Wheat crackers are more sturdy because of the gluten in the grain.

VARIATIONS:

RYE CRACKERS

Use the same recipe as for Wheat Crackers, but use sprouted rye and add ½ cup chia or flaxseed meal and ½ cup water. (The seed meal keeps the crackers from crumbling.)

RICE CRACKERS

Use the same recipe as for Wheat Crackers, substituting sprouted rice for sprouted wheat and add ½ cup chia and ½ cup water.

BUCKWHEAT CRACKERS

Use the same recipe as for Wheat Crackers, substituting sprouted buckwheat for sprouted wheat. If a little seasoning is desired, sprinkle on top of the spread dough before drying. When half dry, mark in 1½ by 2½ inch rectangles. Crackers will then break uniformly when dry.

OAT CRACKERS and BARLEY CRACKERS

Use the recipe for Wheat Crackers and substitute sprouted oats or barley for the wheat. You may add 2 tablespoons of flaxseed or chia seed meal and 2 tablespoons of water may be added to make sturdier, richer crackers.

SWEET RICE WAFERS

Sprout two cups of whole, sweet rice for 72 hours and, substituting it for wheat, proceed the same as for wheat crackers, adding a pinch of salt, a teaspoon of honey and ¼ teaspoon of nutmeg.

"CHEESE" WHEAT CRACKERS

2 cups wheat (left over after third batch of fermec)

¼ cup flaxseed meal

½ teaspoon salt or 1 teaspoon kelp (optional)

water

Blend wheat with enough water to make a thin paste. Add flaxseed and seasoning and blend a few seconds. Drop by spoonfuls on cellophane or plastic wrap and dehydrate; when the up side is dry, turn plastic and crackers over. Peel off plastic and finish drying. The finished, crisp crackers have a pleasant cheese taste.

MILLET CRACKERS

¾ cup millet

¼ cup flaxseed

¾ cup lukewarm water

½ teaspoon salt (optional)

2 teaspoons poppy seed

Sprout millet 48 hours. Sprout flaxseed in the ¾ cup lukewarm water for 12 hours. Do not drain. Store in refrigerator until millet is sprouted. Grind together or mix in blender, adding only enough water to blend well. Add salt and poppy seed. Pour out in thin layer on wax paper or oiled or flour-dusted cookie pan and dehydrate. Mark in triangles when half dry. Break into triangles when crisp and store in cool, dry place.

"FRITO" CORN CURLS

1 cup whole grain corn

½ cup flaxseed

1 cup water

2 tablespoons corn oil (optional)

½ teaspoon salt (optional)

½ teaspoon chili powder (optional)

Sprout grain corn (see sprouting directions). Sprout flaxseed in the 1 cup water for 12 hours. Then store in refrigerator until corn is ready. Fine grind the two together twice. Add corn oil, salt and chili powder. Blend at high speed, adding water. Spread thinly on wax paper or oiled cookie sheet and dehydrate. (See Appendix for oven dehydrating.) When half dry, cut into 1 by 2 inch rectangles and turn over. Pieces will curl as they finish drying. Store in tight container in refrigerator. In a cool dry place they keep for up to ten days.

PASTRY FOR PIES, TARTS and PIZZA

1 cup 24-hour sprouted wheat, finely ground

2 tablespoons oil or melted butter

⅛ teaspoon salt (optional)

Mix together, knead and press into a pie pan, bottom and sides, or tart pans. Place in dehydrator or preheated and turned-off oven until nearly dry, then fill with your favorite pie or tart filling.

EASY, DELICIOUS PIE CRUST VARIATIONS

For a crust for your favorite pie filling treat, try these versatile foods. Simply cover a pie pan with one of the following:

1. 1 cup coconut meal
2. ½ cup coconut
   ½ cup carob
3. 1 cup dehydrated, crumbled soy pulp
4. ½ cup finely chopped dry dates
   ½ cup chopped nuts
5. ½ cup carob mixed with ½ to ¾ cup carrot pulp

PIZZA CRUST

1 cup sprouted buckwheat, finely ground

1 tablespoon soft butter or oil

¼ teaspoon salt or 1 teaspoon kelp (optional)

Double the recipe for 12-inch pizza pan

Knead to a stiff dough. Press into a 9-inch pizza or pie pan. Set aside to dry or dehydrate in warmed, turned-off oven or a dehydrator. When completely dry, fill with raw pizza sauce and top with your favorite embellishments.

Note: This crust is excellent for pies.

TORTILLAS

½ cup cornmeal

½ cup golden flaxseed meal

¼ cup water

½ teaspoon kelp

Mix all and knead. Form into 6 patties, place between 2 sheets of wax paper. Roll to thin circles with a tall glass or jar. Peel off top sheet and leave tortillas at room temperature about 6 hours.

HOLIDAY FRUIT CAKE

Part 1

2 cups sprouted wheat

1 cup dates

1 cup raisins

1 cup sesame seed meal

½ dehydrated orange rind

Part 2

1 cup walnuts, chopped

½ cup carob powder

2 teaspoons kelp

1 teaspoon vanilla

Grind sprouted wheat. Then grind it again with all other ingredients of Part 1. Mix in ingredients of Part 2 and work into a binding dough. Form into a circular cake on a slightly oiled cake plate and set aside for 24 hours. Decorate with nut halves and date slivers. Refrigerate.

CARROT CAKE
(Let it be your entire lunch or dinner)

Part 1
2 cups chopped carrots

1 cup raisins or dates

1 cup 24 to 36-hour
sprouted oats or wheat

Grind all together 2 or 3 times for a fine texture.

Part 2
1 cup fresh wheat bran or rice bran

½ cup soy flour

2 teaspoons kelp

1 cup finely grated coconut or chopped nuts

1 teaspoon cinnamon

¼ teaspoon allspice

Mix these dry ingredients well together.

Part 3
4 tablespoons honey

1 teaspoon vanilla

½ cup raw peanut butter

3 tablespoons water

Mix, then add the ingredients of Parts 1, 2 and 3 and knead until mixture is a firm dough. Make into loaf, place in oiled pan and refrigerate a few hours before slicing and serving with ground coconut or nuts sprinkled over the slices.

NEW LOW-CALORIE CHEESECAKE

2 tablespoons agar

½ cup hot (not boiling) water

½ cup rich almond milk*

3 tablespoons honey

⅛ teaspoon sea salt

1 teaspoon grated lemon rind or ½ and ½ grated lemon and orange rind

2 teaspoons lemon juice

¾ teaspoon pure vanilla

1½ cups sprouted soy cheese (one recipe of soy cheese)

1 teaspoon flaxseed meal

½ cup coconut meal

¼ cup wheat or rice bran

Dissolve agar in water and add the almond milk which has been warmed by sitting over a pan of hot water. Stir well and cool until it begins to thicken. Blend all other ingredients except coconut and bran. Add cooled agar-almond mixture and blend 20 seconds. Combine coconut and bran. Sprinkle half the mixture over bottom of spring form pan. Turn agar mixture into pan and sprinkle with remaining bran-coconut. Chill until firm. Loosen from side of pan with spatula and release cheesecake from spring form onto a chilled plate and refrigerate or serve at once. Serves 6.
Note: This cheesecake is especially delicious served frozen.

* For making almond milk, grind ½ cup almonds in seed mill to fine meal. Blend with ½ cup lukewarm water and strain through fine screenwire sieve.

NUT and SEED BUTTERS and SPREADS

A butter can be made out of any kind of seed or nut or combination of them. In a seed-nut mill, grind just as much as you are going to use for a butter. Once broken down, with the germ exposed to the air, the seed or nut will soon lose come of its nutrients.

One cup of seeds or nuts yields approximately 1½ cups of meal. When mixed with enough water to make a stiff butter, you will have approximately ¾ cup.

We recommend only raw nuts, or slightly sprouted nuts. Both are far more nutritious than roasted ones, and easier to digest, especially the sprouted ones. Almonds and peanuts (legumes) are sprouted in the shell (hull).

For making butters, use a seed-nut mill or grinder with finest disc or, in the case of sprouted seeds or nuts, a blender like the Vita-Mix.

If a kitchen blender such as Osterizer is used, blend the meal with enough water or fermec to make a thick cream, then add a tablespoon or so of flaxseed meal for thickening to the consistency desired.

NUT BUTTER

1 cup nuts ground to meal
3 to 6 tablespoons water

Mix meal and water to a stiff paste. Butter is ready to eat. Enjoy the exquisite, released taste of the nuts.

SEED BUTTER

1 cup seeds ground to fine meal
4 to 6 tablespoons water (sunflower and pumpkin take less water, sesame more, flaxseed the most)

Mix meal and water, adding liquid until desired thickness. Flaxseed butter will thicken much in a few minutes. We season flaxseed and sesame butters with soaked and drained celery seed, caraway, or dill, for instance.

HONEY SOY SPREAD

1 cup 24-hour soaked or 48-hour sprouted soy
4 to 6 tablespoons fermec
4 tablespoons honey
2 tablespoons carob
  Pinch salt

Blend soy and fermec. Pour in dish covered with cloth. Set aside in 75° or 80° for 6 to 10 hours. Stir in honey then carob and salt.

DATE SPREAD

1 cup dates
½ to ¾ cup fermec (use water if spread is to be stored)

Chop finely or grind dates in wheat grass grinder. Mix with fermec to a stiff paste.

FIG-RAISIN JAM

Equal parts ground figs and raisins
Fermec or water

Mix fruits, add enough liquid to make heavy paste

STRAWBERRY JAM

2 cups crushed strawberries
3 to 4 tablespoons honey
2 tablespoons flaxseed meal

Mix and allow a few minutes for thickening. Add more flaxseed meal for thicker jam.

PEAR MARMALADE

1 cup ground, dried pears
Water

Mix just enough water to make a thick paste. If stored, more water may need to be added.

PRUNE PRESERVES

1 cup pitted, ground prunes
Water

Mix prunes and water to make a spreadable paste.

Note: Fruit spreads can be made out of any dried fruits. If too dry, soak overnight and grind. Add a bit of flaxseed meal if preserves are too thin.

VEGETABLE DISHES

Vegetables can be prepared in such a way as to make them a main part of the meal, or as a dish served along with a protein entree. Many can be served warm, a condition that satisfies our taste for a hot, cooked food. Here is a list of recipes that can be served warm. Some can be steam cooked for the transitional diet.

FRESH or FROZEN PEAS

2 cups of fresh peas at room temperature or 2 cups of frozen peas, thawed

¼ teaspoon salt (optional)

1 teaspoon butter

Place the peas in a steamer over hot, not boiling water, set aside in warm place for 15 minutes and serve in a pre-heated bowl. Serves 4 to 6.

Note: Buttered peas (frozen or raw), heated to 104°, are superior in flavor to cooked ones. Peas (fresh or frozen and thawed), with freshly made seed sauce, are delicious served warm or cold. Corn, broccoli, zucchini, cauliflower or a combination of these vegetables may be made the same way. Zucchini is good combined with a strong flavored vegetable as broccoli or asparagus.

BRO-ZUC

1 cup thinly sliced broccoli spears

2 cups thinly sliced zucchini

1 tablespoon warm water

1 tablespoon butter, melted

½ teaspoon salt (optional)

Toss together in double boiler or deep bowl, set in a pan of warm water for 10 minutes, and serve in dish or on plates, preheated. Serves 4 to 6.

OKRA ROYAL

1 avocado, peeled and
  mashed, or 1 cup fresh,
  pureed tomato
1 cup thinly sliced okra
½ cup chopped celery
1 teaspoon kelp

Mix together and serve warm
or cold. (The okra may be
steam cooked 3 minutes. Add
the avocado, chopped celery
and kelp, and serve hot.)
Serves 4 to 6.

CORN ON THE COB
(Everybody's Favorite)

Fresh corn on the cob has the most delicate, sweet taste if the
ears are put in warm water and placed on simmer on the stove, or in
warm water in an electric pot or skillet, set on lowest heat and left
until all reach 104°. (Heat will not harm your finger.) We use a
Corningware covered dish for cooking and serving on the table. Our
guests, not realizing the corn has not been boiled, never fail to
comment on the "superbly fresh" and delicious corn. Butter may be
served with corn.

Note: Buttered corn, cut off the cob or frozen, heated to 104°, like
uncooked corn on the cob, is sweeter and a very special treat.

SQUASH SUPREME

2 cups diced or shredded
  sweet winter squash
2 tablespoons warm water
1 to 2 teaspoons honey
2 teaspoons butter, melted
¼ teaspoon salt
½ teaspoon cinnamon, dash
  of nutmeg (both
  optional)

Blend and serve warm or cold.
(The squash may be steam
cooked until tender, the water
left out and the other ingredients added for a hot, cooked
dish.) Serves 2 to 4.

CABBAGE ROLLS

6 cabbage leaves
½ cup nut butter
½ cup finely chopped or
   ground celery and/or
   carrot
½ cup ground cabbage
1 teaspoon chopped onion
   (optional)

Cut off upper third of cabbage leaves. Grind or finely shred. Mix with nut butter, celery and/or carrot until all stick together. Divide into six portions. Roll one in each leaf and secure with toothpick stuck through the roll. Serve cold or warm. (The cabbage leaves may be steamed for 2 or 3 minutes, the carrot cooked 5 to 8 minutes, and the recipe followed. When the rolls are made, they should be steamed a minute.) Serves 3 to 6.

STUFFED BELL PEPPER

4 bell peppers, halved,
   seeded
1 mashed avocado, or ½
   cup nut or seed butter
¼ cup chopped celery
1 medium beet, shredded
   (or carrot, parsnip, turnip or any combination)
1 to 2 teaspoons kelp
1 tablespoon chopped
   parsley
2 tablespoons sunflower
   seeds, raw or sprouted

Mix all the ingredients but the bell pepper. Fill the pepper shells and top with your favorite salad dressing or sauce. (If you wish this recipe cooked, steam the bell pepper 3 minutes, cook the root vegetable until tender and proceed with the recipe. Do not cook avocado, nut butter, seeds or parsley.) Serves 4 to 8.

CAULIFLOWER-BROCCOLI CASSEROLE

2 cups broccoli cut in small pieces (not chopped)

1 cup cauliflower cut but not chopped

½ teaspoon salt or 1 to 2 teaspoons kelp (optional)

3 tablespoons buckwheat soak water or 1 table-spoon flaxseed meal soaked in ¼ cup water

1 tablespoon butter

Place broccoli and cauliflower in Corningware or Pyrex cooking dish, cover with lid and warm in pan of hot water. Heat the thickened water and butter until the butter is melted. Dribble over the broccoli-cauliflower, season to taste and serve on preheated plates. (Broccoli and cauli-flower can be steamed 3 minutes before making the casserole.) Serves 4 to 6.

ASPARAGUS A-LA-KING

Asparagus

* Almond or sunflower seed cream

Finely chopped red bell pepper, celery, or parsley

Cayenne

Cut asparagus into 1 inch pieces. Pour almond (or sun-flower seed) cream over top. Garnish with the red bell pepper, celery or parsley. Sprinkle lightly with cayenne or your favorite vegetable sea-soning. Serve warm or cold (can be made with 3-minute steamed asparagus).

* Cream is made by thinning almond butter or paste or seed cream with any seed-milk, buckwheat soak water or plain water.

CHINESE VEGETABLES

2 cups finely shredded Chinese cabbage (regular cabbage may be substituted)

½ cup finely sliced water chestnuts or Mexican jicama

½ cup finely sliced (diagonally) celery

½ cup peas, fresh or frozen

½ cup soaked cashew nuts or ½ cup soaked, peeled, sliced almonds

3 teaspoons kelp or ¼ cup soaked dulse

1 large tomato cut in thin wedges

1 cup thick buckwheat soak water or 2 tablespoons flaxseed meal (golden if possible), soaked ½ hour in scant cup of water

1 tablespoon olive oil

Mix all together except for the oil and soak water (or flaxseed meal water). Pour the thickened water over the mixture, toss lightly and top with the tomato wedges. When warmed over hot water and served on preheated plates, this one-dish meal becomes a favorite. (If cooked Chinese vegetables are desired, steam all vegetables except the jicama and tomato. When the other vegetables are cooked, add the warm buckwheat or flaxseed water, the jicama or chestnuts and top with tomato wedges.) Serves 8 to 10.

NEO-SUCCOTASH

2 cups cut-off or frozen corn

1 cup finely cut green beans

2 tablespoons water, preferably thickened with flaxseed meal, or buckwheat soak water

1 tablespoon butter or almond butter

Mix the corn and bean together and warm. Warm the water and butter until butter melts. Dribble over the vegetables and season to taste. (Beans can be steamed 8 to 10 minutes before making the recipe.) Serves 4 to 6.

GARBANZO PATTIES

1 cup garbanzo sprouts
1 cup alfalfa sprouts
2 sprigs parsley
1 medium-sized carrot
¼ cup flaxseed meal
½ to 1 teaspoon celery, poppy, caraway or dill seed
2 tablespoons water

Mix all together and put through a fine grinder, hand mincer or Champion blender. Stir in flaxseed meal and water. Mix well and form into patties to be served cold on a bed of shredded cabbage or lettuce and topped with salad dressing, or warmed and served as an entree with warm sauce. (If you crave this recipe cooked, steam only the carrot, and perhaps the garbanzos. Never cook alfalfa sprouts.) Serves 3 to 4.

PICNIC CROQUETTES

2 cups soy sprouts
1 cup lentil sprouts
½ cup sesame sprouts or cheese
1 cup cut-off or frozen corn
½ cup raw peanut or nut butter
¼ cup flaxseed meal
½ cup chopped celery
1 tablespoon brewer's yeast
2 to 3 teaspoons kelp
1 tablespoon chopped onion (optional)

Finely grind the sprouts, celery and corn. Add other ingredients and mix well. Form into croquettes, roll in any seed or nut meal and store in refrigerator several hours before serving. Can be served cold or warm. (You can steam the soy and lentil sprouts, but nothing else, and proceed with the recipe.) Serves 6 to 8.

ALMOND-MUNG BEAN LOUIE

2 cups mung bean sprouts, slightly chopped

1 cup alfalfa sprouts

½ cup celery, chopped

1 tablespoon dry dulse, crumbled, or 1 teaspoon kelp

¼ cup coarsely chopped nuts

Toss and serve with the following sauce:

½ cup soy, lentil or pea sprouts

½ cup fermented sesame or sunflower sauce

½ cup water or buckwheat soak water or fermec

1 tablespoon oil (optional)

2 small green onions and/or 2 sprigs parsley

Blend all together until creamy. Pour over the tossed ingredients and serve garnished with tomato slices. Serves 4 to 6.

SEED-NUT RAW VEGETABLE LOAF VARIATIONS

After making a few specific seed-nut-vegetable-sprout loaves, croquettes or patties "baked" in the sun or a warm place for a few hours, or stored in the refrigerator until flavors blend and texture sets, try using any combination of similar proportions. Taste variations are limitless. Sometimes the best recipe is a simple one of ingredients on hand. An easy way to serve is to press into a shallow Pyrex baking dish, cut into squares and serve.

Here's an example of what we have served as a tuna-type salad on raw greens, or in a loaf, patties or croquettes, all with suggested variations.

BASIC START SEED-NUT-VEGETABLE RECIPE

½ cup sunflower seed meal

¼ cup water or fermec

2 stalks celery, chopped or ground

1 teaspoon kelp

4 to 6 large mushrooms, chopped

Your favorite vegetable seasonings

Mix and make into loaf, patties, flat casserole or croquettes, or serve in little mounds on a platter of lettuce leaves. Serves 2.

RAW SOUPS

MUSHROOM SOUP

3 cups chopped raw
mushrooms

1½ to 2 cups warm water

¼ teaspoon salt (optional)

1 teaspoon butter and/or
oil (optional) or 2 tablespoons almond butter

Blend. Set blender jar in hot water (not boiling) for 10 minutes. Pour into preheated cream soup cups and serve with a garnish of finely chopped parsley. Serves 2 to 4.

GREEN PEA SOUP

2 cups fresh or frozen peas

1½ cups warm water

¼ teaspoon salt (optional)

1 teaspoon butter and/or
oil (optional)

(Note: 2 tablespoons of
raw cream may be used
instead of the butter and
oil.)

Blend peas and warm water. Pour in top of double boiler and place over very low burner. Do not allow the water to boil. Stir in salt, butter and oil, pour into preheated soup bowls or cups and serve immediately with a sprinkling of celery seed on top. Serves 2 to 4.

Note: Just the peas and water are excellent as a soup which really needs no adornment or flavor additive.

GREEN CREAM OF SPINACH SOUP

1½ cups fresh spinach,
chopped

1½ cups zucchini or summer
squash

1 clove garlic (optional)

¼ teaspoon salt (optional)
or 1 teaspoon kelp

1½ cups warm water

1 teaspoon butter and/or
oil (optional)

Blend vegetables and water. Set blender jar in hot water for 5 to 10 minutes. Put butter and oil in preheated soup cups, add soup and serve. Serves 2 to 4.

SWEET WINTER SQUASH SOUP

2 cups chopped winter
squash

1½ cups warm water

1 teaspoon butter and/or
oil (optional)

1 pinch salt

¼ teaspoon cinnamon (or
bit less)

1 teaspoon honey

Blend. Pour into top of double boiler, let stand until hot (104°) and serve in preheated soup cups. Serves 2 to 4.

PARSNIP SOUP

2 cups unscraped, chopped
parsnips

1½ cups warm water

1 pinch salt

1 teaspoon butter and/or
oil (optional)

1 teaspoon honey

¼ teaspoon mace

Blend at high speed for 30 seconds. Heat to 104° and serve in preheated soup cups. Serves 2 to 4.

BROCCOLI-ZUCCHINI SOUP

1 cup chopped broccoli

2 cups chopped zucchini

1½ cups warm water

¼ teaspoon salt (optional)

1 teaspoon butter and/or
oil (optional)

Blend broccoli, zucchini, salt and water. Set blender jar in pan of hot water for 10 minutes. Preheat soup cups. Put butter and oil in hot cups, pour in the pureed broccoli-zucchini and serve. Serves 2 to 4.

GOLDEN VEGETABLE SOUP

½ cup grated, unscraped carrots

½ cup grated Jerusalem artichokes

1 cup grated crookneck squash

½ teaspoon kelp

1 teaspoon butter and/or oil (optional)

Blend. Place in top of double boiler and set on very low burner until soup is warm (about 104°). Stir and serve in preheated dishes. Serves 2 to 4.

SWEET CORN SOUP (a favorite)

3 large ears of corn, kernels cut off and cobs well scraped for the rich hearts, or 2 cups frozen corn, thawed

1½ cups warm water

¼ teaspoon salt (optional)

1 teaspoon butter and/or oil (optional)

Boil the cobs in the water for 2 minutes. Cool to 104°. Pour over the cut-off corn in the blender. Blend. Set the blender jar in hot water for 10 minutes. Put butter and oil in preheated soup cups, add soup and serve. Serves 2 to 4.

CREAM OF TOMATO SOUP

3 cups raw, pureed tomatoes (with skins)

¼ teaspoon salt

2 tablespoons almond butter

Place ingredients in top of double boiler and set on very low heat until 104°. Stir. Pour into preheated cups, garnish with chopped celery leaves and/or pinch of dried, ground chili pepper. Serves 2 to 4.

SOUPS — WARM and COLD

GAZPACHO SOUP (chilled or warm)

2 cups mashed raw
tomatoes

1 hot chili pepper
(optional)

½ bell pepper

1 large sprig parsley

1 stalk celery with leaves

1 teaspoon onion
(optional)

2 teaspoons kelp or 1 tablespoon soaked dulse

Blend tomatoes for 10 seconds.
Finely chop pepper, parsley,
celery, dulse and onion. Serve
in chilled soup plates with the
chopped vegetables sprinkled
on top, or blend. Can be
warmed and served in pre-
heated soup cups. Serves 2 to 4.

RUSSIAN BEET SOUP (cold or warm)

1 apple-size beet, grated

2 stalks celery, chopped

1 cup mung bean sprouts,
chopped

4 mint leaves, fresh or
dried

½ cup water (seed or nut
soaking water may be
used)

Blend beet, water, mint and
celery. Stir in the mung
sprouts. Garnish with alfalfa
sprouts, chopped watercress or
parsley. Serves 2.

AVOCADO-CAULIFLOWER CREAM SOUP

2 cups chopped cauliflower

1 medium avocado

1 cup water or soaking
water

½ teaspoon salt (optional)
or 1 teaspoon kelp

Blend. Serve in soup dishes
with lemon or lime wedges.
Garnish with dill seed. Serves
2 to 4.

SALADS, SALAD DRESSINGS and MARINATES

"May thy woman be the salad in thy life."
Anonymous

The very word salad brings to mind things bright and beautiful. Everyone loves to gather together the living, sparkling, bright-colored fruits and vegetables to make the most uplifting part of the meal. Traditionally, the meal begins with a salad appealing to the eye and directing attention away from the mundane, the tiresome, the sordid, and focus it upon the joy of anticipation for replenishing the body's energies. The salad accomplishes that. The bright colors excite the imagination and stimulate the appetite.

SALAD MAKINGS and PREPARATIONS

The recipes that follow are suggested combinations of fresh fruits, vegetables and sprouts. Some seasonings and sauces are included. However, since tastes and ideas differ, most of the condiments and sauces are simply listed so that each person may combine and season to his or her own taste.

We rarely make two salads exactly the same. That's the charm of the salad bar way of living. The creation of a salad with eye and taste appeal becomes a joy anticipated and fulfilled every day by each individual.

Choose the freshest fruits and vegetables possible and keep them fresh in the refrigerator or a cool place. Grow your own buckwheat and sunflower sprouts. Then you can cut the plants and put them directly into your salad.

To prepare your fruits and vegetables, wash them in lukewarm water. If you fear they have been sprayed, add an ounce or two of wheat grass juice to a large pan of water and leave the vegetables or fruits in the solution for a couple of minutes. Or add a tablespoon of baking soda to a large pan of water and wash the salad makings. Rinse, then wash again in water to which 2 teaspoons of vinegar have been added.

Salad made from luscious, living products of sun, water and soil will become the most anticipated meal and your main one. Salads, perhaps more than any other food form, lead us to glowing, vibrant health and contentment.

The recipes here are flexible, with ingredients suggested. The amounts can also be altered. The charm of a salad is the result of the love and dedication the salad maker imparts to it. These recipes are to spark your resourcefulness, to inspire you to invent more recipes. You'll have great fun making them, and greater fun creating your own.

A SALAD BAR
FOR YOUR FAMILY and GUESTS

PLATTERS OF GREENS

Beet Tops	Dandelion	Red Lettuce
Lettuce, Bib, Butter and Boston	Endive	Romaine
	Escarole	Radish Tops
Buckwheat Lettuce	Kale	Sorrel
	Lambsquarter	Spinach
Cabbage	Lentil Plants	Sunflower Leaves
Celery Tops	Mint	Watercress
Chard	Parsley	Turnip Tops
Chickweed		
Comfrey		

BOWLS OF SPROUTS

Adzuki Bean	Garbanzo	Sesame
Alfalfa	Lentil	Soy
Celery	Mung Bean	Sunflower
Fenugreek	Oats	Watercress
	Radish	

PLATES OF STEMS AND SHREDDED ROOTS

Asparagus	Jerusalem Artichoke	Rutabaga
Beet	Jicama	Summer Squash
Carrot	Okra	Sweet Potato
Celery	Parsnip	Turnip
Cut-off Corn	Potato	Yam
	Pumpkin	

SALAD ELEGANTS

Avocado Wedges
Bell Pepper
Broccoli Flowers
Cauliflowers
Chives, chopped

Dandelion Buds
Lemon Wedges
Mushrooms
Nasturtium Seeds
(green)

Scallions, chopped
Sea Plants
Spearmint
Tomato Wedges
Zucchini Rings

Note: Dips, Dressings, Oil, Vinegar and Lemon for Salad Bar - See
Section on Salad Dressings

SEED AND HERB SEASONINGS

Cardoman
Caraway
Cayenne
Celery
Chinese Parsley
Cinnamon

Dill
Garlic Powder
Horseradish
Marjoram
Nutmeg

Onion Powder
Parsley
Poppy Seed
Sage
Thyme

APPETIZER SALADS

TOSSED SALAD

1 cup bib (butter) lettuce
1 cup red leaf lettuce
½ cup radishes and tops
½ cup shredded cabbage
½ cup lentil sprouts
2 medium-size tomatoes

Shred or chop each ingredient,
then measure. Toss and serve
with olive oil and apple cider
vinegar. Serves 2 to 4.

SUMMER SALAD NO. 1

2 cups Romaine
1 cup buckwheat lettuce or
   butter lettuce
½ cup fresh peas
½ cup radishes
8 pear (or cherry) tomatoes
2 green onions and tops
   (optional)

Chop and toss. Serve with your favorite dressing or sesame seed dressing. Serves to 4.

SUMMER SALAD NO. 2

2 cups leaf lettuce
½ cup grated carrot
½ cup fresh corn
½ cup alfalfa sprouts
1 teaspoon kelp

Toss and serve with almond cream sauce. Serves 2 to 4.

SUMMER SALAD NO. 3

1 cup grated crookneck
   squash
1 cup mung bean sprouts
½ cup grated yam
½ cup spinach
1 tablespoon soaked dulse
¼ cup grated beet

Toss all but beet. Pour soy mayonnaise or mayonnaise No. 2 over all and sprinkle with the grated beet. Serves 2 to 4.

AUTUMN SALAD NO. 1

2 cups Romaine
½ cup grated Jerusalem
   artichoke or potato
1 cup chopped tomato
1 small avocado, diced
¼ cup sprouted garbanzos,
   marinated
1 tablespoon sweet onion
   (optional)

Toss with olive oil and apple cider vinegar. Serves 2 to 4.

AUTUMN SALAD NO. 2

1 cup chopped cabbage

1 cup grated yam

1 cup clover or alfalfa
sprouts

½ cup sunflower seed
sprouts

Layer salad in order given in individual salad bowls. Top with soy mayonnaise or lemon dressing. Serves 2 to 4.

WINTER SALAD NO. 1

1 cup bean sprouts

1 cup buckwheat lettuce or
celery tops

¼ cup sprouted garbanzos
or soy beans

1 avocado, diced

Chop and toss. Sprinkle with lemon juice and kelp. Serves 2 to 4.

WINTER SALAD NO. 2

1 cup alfalfa sprouts

1 cup buckwheat lettuce or
spinach

½ cup grated parsnip,
potato, turnip or jicama

½ cup mushrooms

1 tablespoon onion or parsley (optional)

Toss and serve with 1 large mashed tomato (fresh or frozen) mixed with a tablespoon of olive oil. Serves 2 to 4.

SPRING SALAD NO. 1

2 cups garden lettuce

1 cup radishes and tops

½ cup dandelion or
lambsquarter

¼ cup black olives, chopped

½ cup sprouted sunflower
seeds

Toss and serve with mayonnaise or your favorite dressing. Serves 2 to 4.

SPRING SALAD NO. 2

2 cups lettuce
1 cup grated carrots and tops, chopped (half-and-half)
1 cup alfalfa or clover sprouts
½ cup chopped comfrey or watercress
1 avocado, diced
1 stalk celery

Toss and sprinkle with lemon juice mixed with 1 tablespoon reconstituted dulse. Serves 2 to 4.

SALAD-OF-THE-SUN

½ cup carrots
½ cup yam or pumpkin
½ cup yellow crookneck squash
½ cup sunflower lettuce or alfalfa sprouts

Grate the vegetables and toss with lettuce or sprouts. We like sesame seed dressing on this salad. Serves 2 to 4.

CORN AND BEAN SALAD

1 cup fresh corn
½ cup chopped celery
½ cup soy sprouts
   Red bell pepper rings

Mix all except pepper rings which are arranged on top. Serve with Thousand Island dressing. (See recipe.) Serves 2 to 4.

TOMATO DELIGHT SALAD

4 medium tomatoes
1 5-inch zucchini
1 stalk celery
½ cup mung bean sprouts
1 tablespoon onion (optional)

Dice tomatoes and zucchini. Slice celery and chop bean sprouts and onion. Mix all and serve with oil and vinegar. Serves 2 to 4.

DANDELION SALAD

1cup dandelions
1cup watercress
1cup bib (butter) lettuce
¼ cup fenugreek sprouts

Toss with oil and lemon or sunflower seed yogurt. Serves 2 to 4.

PARTY SALAD

2 cups Romain lettuce
1 cup adzuki or mung bean sprouts
1 cup watercress or ¼ cup radish tops or ¼ cup radish sprouts
1 cup mushrooms
1 avocado
10 cherry tomatoes, halved

Chop, mix and serve with an assortment of salad dressings, on the side. Serves 6 to 8.

BUFFET SALAD

2 to 4 Jerusalem artichokes, thinly sliced
1 beet, thinly sliced
2 to 4 tomatoes, sliced
Celery sticks
Carrot sticks
Cucumber slices
1 avocado, sliced lengthwise
4 cups alfalfa sprouts

Mound sprouts in center of a large plate or platter. Arrange slices and sticks around it. Serve dressing in separate dish along with shaker of kelp. We suggest sunflower seed sauce. Serves 6 to 8.

ARTICHOKE SALAD

2 artichokes, grated
1 cup carrots, grated
1 cup Chinese cabbage
½ cup comfrey or spinach
  Few mint leaves

Shred cabbage finely, chop mint leaves, comfrey or spinach, and toss with artichokes and carrots. Serve with soy mayonnaise. Serves 4 to 6.

ASPARAGUS SALAD

6 or 8 asparagus spears
1 cup spinach
1 cup mung bean sprouts
½ cup mushrooms
½ cup celery tops

Chop all and mix. Serve with lemon and oil. Serves 4 to 6.

BEET SALAD

1 cup grated beets
1 cup grated apples
1 cup chopped bean
  sprouts

Mix and serve with lemon dressing.

CAULIFLOWER SALAD

2 cups cauliflowerets
1 cup endive
½ cup carrots
1 avocado
½ cup sprouted sesame
  seeds

Chop, mix and serve with a touch of oil, vinegar and kelp. Serves 6.

CABBAGE SALAD

1 cup shredded cabbage
½ cup grated yam
½ cup fresh or dry shredded
  coconut or sprouted
  almonds
1 chopped apple

Mix and serve with lemon dressing. Serves 4.

CARROT SALAD (Children's favorite)

2 cups grated carrots
1 chopped apple
½ cup pineapple
½ cup sprouted wheat
½ cup raisins

Toss and serve with mayonnaise on top or mixed with ingredients. Serves 4 to 6.

CHARD SALAD

2 cups chard, chopped
1 cup celery, chopped
1 tomato
1 avocado
½ cup black olives

Toss chard, olives and celery. Arrange tomato and avocado wedges on top and serve with oil and lime. Serves 4 to 6.

CUCUMBER SALAD

2 6-inch cucumbers
3 firm tomatoes, medium
2 tablespoons finely
  chopped parsley
  Kelp

Slice cucumbers and tomatoes, arrange on salad plates and sprinkle with parsley. Dribble sour cream dressing or soy cream dressing over all. Sprinkle with kelp. Serves 4.

EGGPLANT SALAD

(an excellent and complete lunch)

1 cup shredded or cubed
eggplant

1 cup butter or garden
lettuce

1 cup buckwheat or sun-
flower lettuce

½ cup sprouted rye, oats or
wheat

1 tablespoon chopped
onion (optional)

Toss and serve with Thousand
Island dressing. Serves 4 to 6.

LENTIL SALAD

1 cup sprouted lentils

1 medium size tomato

1 cup Romaine

½ cup celery

½ cup carrots

Finely chop all except the
tomato. Mix. Slice tomato and
arrange on top. Serve with
favorite dressing. Serves 4.

MUSHROOM SALAD

2 cups sliced mushrooms

2 cups chopped sunflower
lettuce or butter lettuce

½ cup fresh or frozen peas

½ cup red sweet bell pepper

Mix and serve with mayon-
naise. Serves 6.

POTATO SALAD (Delicious!)

2 medium potatoes*

2 celery stalks with leaves, chopped

2 tablespoons chopped green nasturtium seeds

1 teaspoon chopped onion (optional)

½ teaspoon salt or 1½ teaspoons kelp

½ cup lecithin mayonnaise

Wash, quarter and steam potatoes 5 minutes. Partially cool. Without peeling, dice. While still slightly warm, mix in mayonnaise. When cool, toss with other ingredients. Serves 4.

* Allowed on transitional diet.

PEPPER SALAD

4 bell peppers

½ cup fresh corn

1 cup alfalfa sprouts

¼ cup fenugreek or wheat sprouts

2 teaspoons lemon juice

½ avocado, mashed

Slice off top of bell peppers and remove seeds. Mix corn, alfalfa, kelp, fenugreek, (chopped) or wheat sprouts, lemon and avocado. Fill bell peppers, top with a dab of mayonnaise and sprinkle with paprika. Serves 4.

PUMPKIN SALAD

1 cup grated pumpkin

1 apple, grated

1 cup cabbage, shredded

½ cup chopped walnuts

Toss and serve with Lemon dressing. Serves 6 to 8.

SPINACH SALAD

3 cups chopped spinach

½ cup soy sprouts

8 or 10 cherry tomatoes

1 teaspoon celery seed

Halve tomatoes. Toss all and serve with oil and vinegar or your favorite dressing. Serves 4 to 6.

TURNIP SALAD

1 cup grated turnip
½ cup sliced water chestnuts
½ cup grated zucchini
1 cup mung bean sprouts
½ cup celery leaves, or Chinese parsley, chopped

Toss and serve with 2 tablespoons oil, 2 tablespoons lemon juice and 1 teaspoon honey. A light sprinkling of ginger gives salad an exotic flavor. Serves 4 to 6.

WATERCRESS SALAD

2 cups watercress
2 cups mung bean or alfalfa sprouts
½ cup sunflower seeds, sprouted
½ cup mushrooms

Chop if desired, toss and serve with Thousand Island dressing or soy cheese dressing. Serves 4 to 6.

ZUCCHINI SQUASH SALAD

1 cup sliced zucchini
½ cup sliced crookneck squash
1 cup shredded leaf lettuce
½ cup grated carrot
½ cup chopped chives

Toss and serve with favorite dressing. Serves 4 to 6.

ONE-TWO-THREE SALADS

Salads need not depend on a lot of different ingredients for excellence. Famous chefs of Florence, Italy, where gourmet cooking flourished in the early Christian era, considered a salad of tiny lettuce leaves alone, with a wine-honey dressing, to be the epitome of salad delicacy and eating joy.

The following recipes are made with one, two or three vegetables. They are our favorites. We do not suggest a dressing, but you may choose your own. We serve the salads with lemon or nothing at all, enjoying the exquisite, subtle flavors of the crisp, unadorned, living food.

SOME "THREE" SALADS WE ENJOY

NO. 1	NO. 2
Carrots	Alfalfa Sprouts
Apples	Mushrooms
Pecans	Tomatoes

NO. 3	NO. 4
Cucumber	Jerusalem Artichokes
Zucchini	Asparagus
Onion	Avocado

NO. 5	NO. 6
Leaf or Butter Lettuce	Cabbage
Parsley	Carrots
Tomato	Bell Pepper

NO. 7	NO. 8
Romaine	Celery
Okra	Garbanzo Sprouts
Fresh Horseradish	Cherry Tomato

"TWO" SALADS

NO. 1	NO. 2
Alfalfa Sprouts Avocado	Adzuki Bean Sprouts Celery

NO. 3	NO. 4
Lentil Sprouts Tomato	Beet Apple

NO. 5	NO. 6
Red Lettuce Okra	Zucchini Sesame Seed Sprouts

NO. 7	NO. 8
Butter Lettuce Young Dandelion Leaves	Sunflower Lettuce Crookneck Squash

"ONE" SALADS

NO. 1	NO. 2
Mung Bean Sprouts	Buckwheat Lettuce

NO. 3	NO. 4
Alfalfa Sprouts	Sunflower Lettuce

NO. 5	NO. 6
Clover Sprouts	Yam, sliced or cut in sticks

NO. 7	NO. 8
Jicama, sliced	Halves of Avocado-in-the-skin

NO. 9	NO. 10
Butter Lettuce	Grated Turnip

A garden salad can become a full meal by increasing the portion served or by adding some hearty ingredient like soy sprouts or garbanzo sprouts, sunflower or sesame seed sprouts, sprouted cereal grains or nut meats, root vegetables or avocado, topped with a seed yogurt or seed meal dressing. Such a salad becomes a dinner and, as a heavy meal, is better eaten in the middle of the day. If, however, the largest meal of necessity can come only in the evening, it should be eaten as early as possible. For most people, some form of mild exercise should be taken three or four hours after eating and before retiring.

SALAD DRESSINGS and MARINATES

Some natural seasonings that may be added to salad dressings: paprika, curry powder, chili powder, dried and ground papaya seed (a mild pepper), anise seed, parsley (dried or fresh), mint leaves (dried or fresh), nutmeg, fresh grated ginger, or any of the natural spices, used sparingly, or any combination of seasoning.

MAYONNAISE NO. 1

½ cup lemon (lime juice or apple cider vinegar)

3 tablespoons seed or nut butter

¼ cup oil

1 teaspoon kelp

Blend the lemon and seed or nut butter. At low speed add oil slowly. If you want a thinner or thicker mayonnaise, add less or more oil. Store in glass jar in the refrigerator.

VARIATION:

FRESH THOUSAND ISLAND DRESSING

To the Mayonnaise No. 1 recipe add a pureed, medium-size, ripe tomato. A dash each of celery salt and onion powder, or your favorite herbal seasonings may be added.

MAYONNAISE NO. 2

½ cup golden flaxseed meal

¼ cup lemon juice or apple cider vinegar

¼ cup water

¼ cup oil

2 teaspoons honey

¼ teaspoon salt or 1 teaspoon kelp

¼ teaspoon dry mustard

Blend at low speed and add oil gradually. This can be made with an egg beater or electric mixer. Store in refrigerator.

LECITHIN MAYONNAISE

2 tablespoons liquid lecithin

½ cup oil

1 teaspoon lemon juice

¼ teaspoon honey

½ teaspoon kelp

With fork or small egg beater, mix lecithin and oil. Add lemon, few drops at a time. Add honey and kelp and beat until very creamy. Store in refrigerator.

TERRA SALAD DRESSING

½ cup sesame or sunflower
   seed meal

½ cup fermec

½ cup carrot, beet or celery
   juice

1 tablespoon reconstituted
   dulse

2 teaspoons kelp

1 teaspoon onion or button
   garlic (optional)

¼ cup oil

   Herb seasonings to taste

Blend all together and serve
over sliced tomatoes, avocado
or any green salad or shredded
vegetables.

AVOCADO DRESSING

1 avocado, mashed

2 tablespoons lemon, lime
   or apple cider vinegar

1 teaspoon kelp powder or
   ¼ teaspoon salt

Mix thoroughly and serve over
salad or store in the refrigerator for up to 12 hours.

ALMOND CREAM DRESSING

1 cup almond meal

1 cup water

1 tablespoon flaxseed meal

   Dash of cayenne
   (optional)

Blend until creamy. If too
thick, add more water. Makes
about 1½ cups dressing. For
fruits, season with orange
peel, or favorite fruit
seasoning.

LEMON DRESSING

3 tablespoons lemon juice

2 tablespoons honey

4 tablespoons thick
   slippery elm water or
   flaxseed or buckwheat
   soak water

Beat with a fork until foamy
or blend. Makes dressing for 4
servings of salad. Serve on
fruits and some vegetable
salads.

FRUIT SALAD DRESSING

¾ cup fruit juice (apple, orange or pineapple)

2 tablespoons coconut meal

1 tablespoon oil (optional)

1 teaspoon honey

Mix all together by hand or blend. Serve over any single raw fruit, or combination of cut-up fruits. Makes enough dressing for 4.

Note: Fruit salad dressings can be made with any combination of fruit juices and nut butters. Our favorite is made with orange or pineapple juice and almond butter.

BERRY DRESSING

2 cups of berries, fresh or frozen (strawberries, blackberries, raspberries, loganberries, etc.)

1 to 2 tablespoons honey

Puree berries in blender at low speed, remove seeds with screen wire colander, and if desired, add honey and stir. Serve chilled over sliced bananas, apples or pears. Serves 4 to 6.

SOY MAYONNAISE

1 cup soy cheese

1 tablespoon oil (optional)

2 teaspoons lemon juice

1 teaspoon honey

½ cup water

Blend or whip by hand. Store in refrigerator. Keeps up to a week. Makes 1¾ cups.

EPICUREAN SALAD DRESSING

1 cup nut meal or seed meal
or any combination, as
pecans and flax, filberts
and sesame, black wal-
nuts and sunflower, etc.

2 cups mashed or pureed
tomatoes

¼ cup washed and drained
dulse

½ cup celery tops and/or
parsley

Blend or finely chop celery or
parsley and mix all together
by hand. Store in the refrigerator. Keeps 2 days. Makes 2
cups.

SOY CREAM DRESSING

½ cup heavy, sprouted soy
milk

2 teaspoons lemon juice
Pinch salt

1 tablespoon sunflower
seed cheese

Mix and season to taste. Serve
immediately.

SOUR CREAM DRESSING

Plain, raw sour cream makes an excellent dressing by itself.
However, seasonings may be added to fit the individual taste.

MARINATES

TOMATO MARINATE

1 cup raw tomato juice
2 tablespoons lemon juice
1 tablespoon tamari sauce
½ teaspoon celery seeds
½ teaspoon caraway

Mix together and pour over mushrooms, sprouted garbanzos, sprouted soy beans, cauliflower or eggplant, etc. Allow to marinate at least an hour. Several hours is better. Makes enough for 4 to 6 vegetable servings.

VINEGAR MARINATE

½ cup vinegar
½ cup water
¼ cup olive oil
1 tablespoon reconstituted dulse
2 teaspoons kelp
1 teaspoon dill seed

Mix and let sit half an hour, stirring occasionally. Marinate vegetables with the sauce for 1 to 4 hours. Enough for 4 to 6 vegetable servings.

OIL AND VINEGAR MARINATE

½ cup vinegar
¼ cup olive oil
1 tablespoon tamari sauce

Mix and pour over a cup of sprouted garbanzos and store in refrigerator. Use a few tablespoons of garbanzos on salads. Marinated garbanzos keep several days.

We are all different and must fit eating habits to our own needs. For instance, Elizabeth eats the same amount for breakfast, lunch and dinner, with a half meal of sub-acid fruit as a before-bed snack. Elton eats a light (or no) breakfast, a moderate lunch and a large, main-meal salad at night with only a rare night time snack of fruit and a few nuts. Neither of us is overweight. In fact, according to the charts, we are both slightly underweight. Nevertheless, such eating habits allow us high energy and a very real sense of well-being.

These recipes, starting you on your new adventure in eating, living and enjoying, will do the same for you.

CHEESE AND YOGURT
(cultured with fermec)

In the 19th century, farm folk made a fermented wheat or barley drink they called Poor Man's Beer. It was not only pleasantly refreshing, but highly nutritious as well since it contained B vitamins and minerals. And the acidophilus culture provided good flora for maintaining healthy intestines. Such nonalcoholic beer can still be bought in Scandinavia.

We call this Poor Man's Beer fermec. Before making cheeses and yogurt, you will make the sprouted wheat, fermented culture called fermec upon which it depends.

FERMEC (culture)

1 cup wheat berries

1½ cups water

Wash and drain. Add water and soak 12 hours. Drain, saving the water for other recipes or for drinking. Rinse well and turn jar upside down at a 45° angle for another 12 hours, rinsing a time or two. Grind sprouted seeds. Put 4 rounded tablespoons of the ground wheat in a quart jar and fill with lukewarm water. Allow to stand, topped with cheesecloth or nylon net or screen and secured by a rubber band, for three days. The fourth day the fermec is ready for making cheese. (We make fermec in 24 hours by setting it just above the electric baseboard heater in 90° temperature.) Do not throw wheat away. Fill the wheat jar again with lukewarm water and set aside at room temperature for 24 hours. Pour fermec off in a jar for your nutritious drink through the day and repeat the fermec making process one more time.

Note: The pure starch left after liquid fermec is poured off may be used. The starch is mostly converted to invert sugars (fructose) and is quite nutritious and digestible. Use as you would cream, in cream soups, creamy salad dressings or seed cheese dips. If dried or nearly so, it is good as a thickening agent for sauces. After three jars of fermec have been produced, the wheat left may be composted or made into fermec "cheese" crackers (see section on **Breads**).

FLAXSEED CHEESE (Our favorite for travel)

3 cups flaxseed meal (2 cups seeds)

1¼ to 1½ cups fermec

2 teaspoons kelp

Mix together, knead, work into a "log" roll on a breadboard sprinkled with flaxseed meal. Roll in wax paper and set aside for 24 to 48 hours. Refrigerate. Slice for serving. Flaxseed will keep up to three weeks, even out of refrigeration if kept tightly rolled in plastic wrap, in temperatures under 80°.

SUNFLOWER SEED CHEESE

3 cups sunflower seed meal (2 cups seed)

2 teaspoons kelp

¾ cup fermec (more for a softer cheese)

Mix together, knead well and pack into covered dish. We like Corningware, square covered dishes. Or make into a roll and wrap in cellophane or plastic wrap. Set aside in the kitchen for 24 to 36 hours. Mold may appear on the top of dish but it is good and adds to the flavor. However, for guests, you may want to scrape it and the darkened top off. Serve from the dish at the table, or slice from roll. It will keep in the refrigerator for a week to 10 days.

SESAME SEED CHEESE

3 cups sesame seed meal (2 cups seed)

2 to 3 teaspoons kelp

½ to 1 cup fermec, or more (the more finely ground, the more moisture needed)

Mix all together and knead. Press into a covered dish and set aside for 24 to 48 hours. The mold that will begin to form on the top is good to eat (tangy), but may be scraped off. Refrigerate. Serve in slices with sprouted grain crackers. **Note:** Mold can be stirred back into the cheese (if not too firm) giving a blue cheese flavor.

SUNFLOWER SEED YOGURT or DIP

2 cups sunflower seed sprouts (12-18 hours)

2 teaspoons kelp

½ to ¾ cup fermec

or

1 cup sunflower seed, ground to fine meal

1 cup fermec, mixed together and set aside to ferment 6-10 hours (longer for a more aged taste).

Blend all together at medium speed. Or, if mixture becomes too thick, add a little more fermec. Pour into a dish, cover with cloth and set aside for 24 hours. This yogurt, if quite thick, makes an excellent dip which can be seasoned with celery seeds, onion, parsley or dill seed. If thinned to a cream, it can be used as any other yogurt, plain, with fruit or as a salad dressing.

VARIATIONS:
SESAME SEED YOGURT

Sesame yogurt can be made the same as sunflower yogurt, either recipe, with a little more fermec added since the sesame seeds are drier than sunflower seeds.

PUMPKIN SEED YOGURT and DIP

Follow the same directions as for sesame seed yogurt and dip. The plain, natural rich flavor of the seeds calls for little or no additional seasoning. Serve as dip, dressing or thinned with a little fermec sauce.

FLAXSEED YOGURT

1½ cups flaxseed meal
2 teaspoons kelp
1¼ cups fermec
or
1 cup of 48-hour jar-sprouted flaxseed
½ to ¾ cups fermec
2 teaspoons kelp

Blend all together at medium speed. If mixture thickens more than cream, add more fermec and blend a few seconds more. Pour into covered dish and set aside for 12 to 24 hours. The consistency is like syrup. This yogurt is good as an entree sauce, fruit or vegetable salad dressing, or eaten as plain dip with crackers.

VARIATION:

CHIA SEED YOGURT

Follow the directions for making flaxseed yogurt. Chia seed yogurt is especially good as a green salad dressing.

SESAME SEED YOGURT and DIP

2 cups sesame seed meal
¾ to 1 cup fermec
2 to 3 teaspoons kelp
or
2 cups sesame, sprouted 48 hours
¾ cup fermec
3 teaspoons kelp

Blend, pour into dish, cover and set aside for 24 to 48 hours. The bit of mold on top can be stirred in for blue cheese flavor or removed. To thicken for dip if too thin, stir in a tablespoon of flaxseed meal. This yogurt has a fuller, aged flavor and is delicious on sprouted grain crackers, zucchini slices or walnut halves. Parsley, finely chopped, may be added, or raw pureed tomato to make salad dressing.

SOY FARMER CHEESE

2 cups of soy beans
  sprouted until sprouts are
  length of beans
3 cups water
3 tablespoons lemon juice

Blend soy beans and water or fine-grind beans, add water, stir well. In cheesecloth, squeeze out the soy milk. Place in double boiler, stirring occasionally, until about 120°. (You can't quite stand your finger in it.) Remove from stove and add lemon juice, stirring the minimum. Strain through double cheesecloth-lined colander. When most of whey has drained off, lift corners of cheesecloth, tie together and hang to finish draining. In 90 minutes, all whey will have drained off and your ball of nutritious, delicious and versatile soy cottage cheese is ready to slice and eat, or make into a salad dressing that tastes like mayonnaise (see Salad Dressings and Sauces).

Note: If lemon juice is added to the soy milk *before* heating, the result will be cottage cheese which tastes much the same but has more texture.

The pulp left over from cheese-making is delicious when used in entree dishes, sprinkled on salads (it will keep 2 or 3 days in the refrigerator) or dehydrated and crumbled to be used in raw granola, as croutons on salads and garnishes on soups, vegetable dishes, nut loaves, patties, etc. Since the pulp is from sprouts, it can be mixed with almost any food. It's taste is mild and rich. You'll find many uses for it besides putting it on the compost. The whey is also nutritious. Drink or put on houseplants, garden or compost. Whey tastes like buttermilk.

UNHEATED, RAW TOFU

2 cups soy beans
½ cup fermec

Soak beans 24 hours or sprout them 48 hours. Add water and blend or grind beans and stir in the fermec. Strain through double cheesecloth, pressing out milk. Pour in a small, deep dish, set in warm place overnight or 8-10 hours or until tofu sets up (coagulates).

SWEETS, TREATS and DRIED FRUIT

PRUNE PARFAIT

2 cups pitted 24-hour
    soaked prunes
2 oranges, peeled and
    sectioned
1 teaspoon honey
    (optional)
    Coconut

Blend prunes, orange and honey until smooth as thick cream. (If mixture is too heavy for blender, add more orange.) Serve in parfait glasses and sprinkle with grated coconut. Serves 6 to 8.

THANKSGIVING CRANBERRY FRUIT CUP

1 lb. of fresh cranberries, ground

2 large or 4 small apples, unpeeled, (if unsprayed) and grated

2 tablespoons flaxseed meal

4 to 6 tablespoons honey

2 cups frozen or fresh blueberries

½ cup chopped pecans or walnuts

Mix together cranberries, apples, flaxseed and honey. Stir in blueberries. Serve in fruit dishes, sprinkle with chopped nuts, chill and serve. (The flaxseed meal thickens the juice slightly.) Serves 12.

PERSIMMON PUDDING

4 large or 6 small ripe persimmons

1 papaya, small Hawaiian Pumpkin seeds, coarsely chopped

Blend persimmons with papaya at low speed until smooth. Pour into sherbet dishes and garnish with chopped pumpkin seeds. Chill. Serves 4 to 6.

DATE DARKO

1 cup seeded, sticky dates

½ cup fermec or water

½ cup apple juice (pear or pineapple juice)

½ cup chopped nuts (walnuts, pecans or filberts)

Blend all but nuts at low to medium speed. Stir in nuts, pour into dishes (or tart shells), chill and serve with a sliver of raw sweet yam (curled in cold water) on top. Serves 2 to 4.

RAISIN PUDDING

1 cup drained, 48-hour
  sprouted wheat, buck-
  wheat or rice
1 cup pineapple or apple
  juice
1 teaspoon slippery elm
  powder
¼ cup carob powder
½ cup raisins
  Pinch salt

Blend wheat and juice to
medium cream, stir in carob
and slippery elm powder until
smooth, then add raisins. Chill
for several hours or overnight.
Serve in custard cups with a
large raisin on top.
Serves 4 to 6.

WATERMELON-CANTALOUPE PLATE

Watermelon
Cantaloupe
Pumpkin seeds, chopped

On salad plates, arrange inch
cubes of watermelon and cantaloupe. Sprinkle with pumpkin seeds. Serve immediately.
(This is a great summer tea
time treat.)

Note: Pumpkin, cantaloupe and watermelon belong to the same
botanical family. A few seeds of the family combine with this salad.

PEAR-BANANA DESSERT

4 medium bananas
4 medium pears
1 teaspoon honey
  (optional)

Peel and slice bananas, peel
and slice pears, cutting sec-
tions in two. Add slightly
warmed honey dribbled over
all, and mix. We serve in
green glass fruit dishes. Sprinkle with coconut. Serves 4.

CRAN-APPLE SAUCE

4 medium red apples, cored and grated or chopped

1 cup fresh cranberries

1 cup apple juice

1 to 2 tablespoons honey

Cranberry halves soaked in honey water

Sprigs of parsley

Blend apples, cranberries, apple juice and honey until quite smooth. Pour into sauce dishes, top with red cranberry half and parsley sprig, and serve at once. Serves 4 to 6.

CAROB "CHOCOLATE" PUDDING

(Children's favorite)

1¼ cups sprouted buckwheat

1 cup buckwheat soak water or plain water

1 tablespoon oil (sesame, soy, safflower or sunflower)

2 tablespoons honey

1 rounded tablespoon flax-seed meal

1 teaspoon vanilla

1 teaspoon liquid lecithin (optional)

¼ teaspoon salt or 1 tea-spoon kelp

⅔ cup carob, sifted

Mix oil and lecithin together. Blend this mixture with the buckwheat, soak water, honey, salt and vanilla until a thick cream. Mix carob and flaxseed, then add gradually and blend. Pour into pudding dishes or sherbet glasses and sprinkle with coconut or chopped cashews. Chill. Serves 4.

BANANA-DATE PUDDING

1 cup ground dates

1 cup sprouted soy pulp or carrot pulp

1 cup fermec or water

1 cup chopped nuts or coconut meal

2 tablespoons flaxseed meal or 1 tablespoon slippery elm powder

2 or 3 bananas

Mix dates, pulp, liquid, flax-seed meal or slippery elm powder by hand or blender until it is creamy and foamy. Sprinkle half the nuts over the bottom of a 9-inch square Pyrex baking dish. Pour the date mix over the nuts, slice the bananas on it and top with the rest of the nuts. Refrigerate a few hours to set up. Serve in squares. Serves 8 to 9.

BANANA ICE CREAM (No. 1)

6 large or 8 medium bananas

Peel and freeze on pan, small tray or in plastic bag. Five or ten minutes before serving, remove from freezer. When ready to serve, slice into four to six sauce dishes. Serve plain. For a festive dessert, sprinkle with chopped nuts or with "chocolate" carob pudding spooned over them, or puree of any kind of berries, chilled. Serves 6 to 8.

BANANA ICE CREAM (No. 2)

6 bananas, frozen, sliced

1 cup sprouted grain milk (see page 173 for buckwheat, rice, oats or barley milk)

1 to 2 teaspoons honey

2 tablespoons oil

Dissolve honey in grain milk. Place all ingredients in blender and whirl until a thick cream. Serve immediately in ice cold dishes. Serves 4 to 6.

BANANA ICE CREAM (No. 3)

(for old-fashioned hand or electric ice cream freezer)

12 large ripe bananas
3 tablespoons honey
2¾ cups grain milk (see page 173 for grain milks)
4 tablespoons oil

or

12 large ripe bananas
2 cups grain milk
1 cup thick raw cream

Dissolve honey in grain milk. Add oil or raw cream and mashed bananas, stir well and pour in freezer for freezing. When frozen, serve in chilled dishes or store in the freezer. Makes approximately 1 quart of fluffy ice cream.

BANANA MARBLE ICE CREAM (No. 4)

6 large bananas, frozen on a tray or in a cellophane bag
2 cups any frozen berries

Feed the bananas, one at a time, in the grinder, with a chilled dish to catch the finished ice cream. When the banana is nearly ground, add a few frozen strawberries, raspberries or blueberries for marbling. Serve at once. Serves 6.

DATE SHERBET

1 cup pitted dates, soaked several hours in ½ cup of buckwheat soak water or plain water
½ cup fruit juice (apple, pineapple, pear or orange)
¼ cup chopped nuts
1 tablespoon oil (optional)

Blend all except nuts at high speed until foamy (about 30 seconds). Freeze in tray. A couple of hours before serving, remove from freezer, put in bowl, mash until stiff cream, add nuts, return to freezer and leave until ready to serve. Serves 4.

SHERBETS AND ICE CREAMS

(Made with a Champion mixer-grinder)

Any frozen fruits can be made into sherbets and ice creams by following the same general directions as in the Date Sherbet recipe. Remember, freezing makes fruits taste sweeter and no sweetener need be added. The longer one is on the raw-food diet, the less one craves sweets. We seldom add honey to fruits. Cranberries and raw rhubarb are the exceptions.

VARIATION:

Put 2 cups of any frozen fruit in the blender, add 1 cup of raw cream, sweet or sour, or 1 cup of heavy soy milk and 1 tablespoon of oil, honey to taste, and blend, using stomper. Some frozen fruits may need more liquid, some less. Serve at once in chilled dishes.
Note: If honey is used, dissolve in the liquid before blending.

CINNAMON COOKIES

1 cup 24-hour sprouted
 oats, ground twice

2 tablespoons flaxseed meal

¼ cup carob flour

1½ teaspoons kelp

2 tablespoons honey

¾ teaspoon cinnamon

1 cup pitted, ground dates

1 teaspoon vanilla

1 to 2 tablespoons water

Mix all together and knead well. Roll out ½ inch thick and cut in squares or with cookie cutter. Dust with carob powder.
Note: 1 or 2 tablespoons of brewer's yeast may be added to any cookie recipe for extra protein and Vitamin B nutrition.

PEANUT BUTTER COOKIES

1 cup raw peanut butter

2 cups sprouted oats, barley or wheat, ground twice

¼ cup carob powder, preferably raw

1 to 2 teaspoons kelp

1 cup of dates, pitted and ground or 1 cup dried pears, ground

Rice bran

Mix all together except carob powder and knead. If not stiff enough, add rice bran. Roll out on oiled cookie sheet dusted with carob. Cut into rectangles 1½ x 2 inches and allow to dry a few hours, then store in the refrigerator.

RAISIN SPICE COOKIES

2 cups ground raisins

2 cups 24-hour sprouted barley, wheat, oats or buckwheat

½ cup chopped pecans

¼ teaspoon salt or 1½ teaspoons kelp

½ teaspoon each cinnamon, nutmeg and allspice

Carob powder

Mix all together except carob powder and knead well to make a stiff, adhering dough. Pat to ½ inch thick on cookie sheet dusted with carob powder. Dust the top with carob, cut in squares and store in refrigerator (or cookie jar for a few days).

DATE COCONUT COOKIES

2 cups pitted, ground dates (tightly packed)

2 cups finely ground coconut

Coconut meal

Mix all together except coconut meal and knead. (Mixture will be *very* stiff.) Make into 2 rolls 1½ to 2 inches in diameter. Roll in coconut meal, set aside for 24 hours, slice in ⅜ inch thick rounds and store in refrigerator.

RAISIN BARS

2 cups ground raisins

2 cups sunflower seed meal

1 cup 24-hour sprouted
  wheat or buckwheat,
  ground, or the wheat left
  after the fermec is poured
  off (drain wheat well)

¼ teaspoon salt or 1 tea-
  spoon kelp

1 teaspoon honey

  Water

  Soy or carob powder

Mix all together except water,
soy or carob powder, and
knead to stiff, adhering dough,
adding water only if necessary.
Press into a 9 x 14 inch, oiled
baking dish, dust with soy or
carob powder and set aside for
24 hours. Cut in 1 x 2 inch
bars. These cookies can be
stored outside the refrigerator
for a week.

CAROB "CHOCOLATE" COOKIES

2 cups twice-ground com-
  frey root

2 cups of finely ground
  coconut

1 teaspoon vanilla

⅛ teaspoon salt or ½ tea-
  spoon kelp

1 cup carob powder

4 tablespoons honey

  Water to make a stiff
  dough (2 to 6
  tablespoons)

Mix all together and knead.
Divide in half and work into
two rolls 1½ inches in diameter on a breadboard covered
with carob powder. Set aside
to dry for 24 hours and store
in the refrigerator. Slice as
needed.

PRUCHI COOKIES

1 cup 24-hour soaked and pitted prunes

½ cup chia seed meal (flaxseed meal can be substituted)

½ cup prune soak water

1 tablespoon honey

1 teaspoon kelp

1½ cups oatmeal, powdered

½ teaspoon vanilla

1 cup finely chopped nuts

Wheat or rice bran or powdered oatmeal

Blend the prunes, water, honey and kelp until creamy. Add oatmeal, chia seed meal and nuts and knead to a stiff dough. If not quite stiff enough, add more oatmeal or rice bran. Press into a 9 x 11 inch baking dish sprinkled with bran. Top with sprinkling of bran. Set aside for 24 hours. Cut in 1 x 2 inch pieces and store in refrigerator.

FLAXSEED SESAME BARS

½ cup flaxseed meal

1 cup sesame seeds

2 cups oatmeal flour (rolled oats ground or dry-whirled in the blender) or fresh-ground hulless oats

½ teaspoon baking soda, or potassium bicarbonate

2 tablespoons brewer's yeast (grown on molasses)

3 tablespoons honey or raw sugar

¼ teaspoon salt or 2 teaspoons kelp (optional)

2 teaspoons vanilla

1 to 1½ cups fermec

Mix dry ingredients, add liquids and make into a stiff dough. If too stiff for working, add more liquid. Flour breadboard or cookie pan with oat flour and roll or pat the cookie dough to ¼ to ½ inch thickness. Dust with oat flour and leave at room temperature 24 hours. Cut in rectangles. Store in tight container in refrigerator.

Sugarless candies can be made from any combination of dried sweet fruits, nuts and seeds. You'll have fun creating all sorts of delicious recipes. When buying dried fruits select unsulfured ones. They will be brown in color.

CRAZY CAROB CARAMELS

1½ cups flaxseed meal
2 tablespoons honey
1 cup water or soak water
½ cup pitted, ground dates
1 pinch salt (optional)
¾ cup carob powder

Dissolve honey in water. Add other ingredients and mix to a stiff dough. Work into 1½ inch roll on a breadboard dusted with sifted carob powder. Set aside, covered with a cloth for 4 to 6 hours. Slice and serve or store in refrigerator.

FIG CARAMELS

3 cups figs, ground
1 cup flaxseed meal
1 to 2 tablespoons honey
4 to 6 tablespoons orange, pineapple or apple juice
⅛ teaspoon salt

Mix together, knead well and make into a sausage roll. Wrap in cello-wrap and refrigerate. Slice for serving. **Note:** If figs are very dry, more moisture may be needed.

RAI-SEE BARS

(This is our favorite, and so simple!)

2 cups seedless raisins, ground
2 cups sesame seed meal

Mix and knead. (Very stiff.) Press firmly into an oiled stainless steel or iron cookie pan. Set aside 24 hours. Cut in bars and store in refrigerator.

NEW FIG NEWTONS

2 cups figs

2 cups sprouted wheat (or other sprouted grain)

¾ cup nuts

⅛ teaspoon salt or ½ teaspoon kelp (optional)

1 tablespoon honey or blackstrap molasses (optional)

Grind all together, knead like dough, form into walnut-size balls or make into roll for slicing. Set aside for 24 hours. Finished balls or rolls can be dusted with brown rice polish or finely ground wheat bran. Store in refrigerator.

PRUNE PLOPS

2 cups of 24-hour soaked prunes, pitted and chopped or ground

1 cup sprouted and ground buckwheat or rice

¾ cup chopped almonds

¾ cup flaxseed meal

½ teaspoon salt or 1½ teaspoons kelp

Mix and knead, press into oiled cookie pan and set aside for 24 hours. Cut in squares and dust with whole grain rice flour. Store in refrigerator.

SESAME-RAISIN CIRCLES

2 cups raisins, ground

2 cups brown sesame seed meal

2 cups finely ground sprouted oats (or wheat, buckwheat, rye, rice millet or barley)

1 tablespoon honey

Mix and knead until smooth and firm. Make into small balls or circles, roll in whole sesame seeds, arrange on oiled cookie sheet and set aside for 24 hours. Store in cookie jar in a cool place or refrigerator.

PECAN DELIGHT

1 lb. pitted dates

2 cups nut meal (pecan, walnut, filbert, almond or coconut)

Mix and knead well. The mass will be *very* firm. Divide. Work into 1½ inch diameter "sausages". Roll on breadboard sprinkled with rice polish or soy flour. Arrange on cookie sheet and leave in cool room for 24 hours. Slice and store in cool dry place or refrigerator.

CAROB "CHOCOLATE" RINGS

¾ cup sifted carob flour

1½ cups flaxseed meal

½ cup honey

1 teaspoon vanilla

⅛ teaspoon salt (optional)

Warm water to make a *stiff* dough

Mix and knead. Make into two rolls about 1½ inches in diameter. Roll in rice polish or soy flour spread thinly on the breadboard. Allow to dry 24 hours. Slice and store in cool place.

DRIED FRUITS

Dried fruits are delicious sweet treats (dates, figs, raisins, pineapples, bananas, apples, pears, apricots, peaches, prunes). They can be eaten as is, in which case they must be thoroughly chewed and mixed with saliva to be reconstituted before swallowing. Or they can be soaked in water at room temperature for 24 hours, then eaten as fresh fruit sauce.

Prunes, soaked and drained (or unsoaked), and dates make irresistable sweet treats when the pits are removed and a nut (pecan or walnut half, almond, filbert, cashew or Brazil nut) is put in the pit's place.

Any dried fruit (single or in combination) can be ground and mixed with any seed or nut meal or fine coconut (with or without chopped nuts), and formed into rolls for slicing, or thin sheets for cutting into squares, or balls or circles. Such confections can be rolled in or sprinkled with pulverized oatmeal, seed meal, powdered coconut, arrow root flour, brown rice flour or soya flour. If a confection needs to be sweeter, add honey, black molasses, pure maple syrup, barley syrup, carob, date sugar, cinnamon **bark** liquor (made by boiling cinnamon bark in a little water and using where a bit of liquid and flavor is needed) or fructose. Dried papaya, bananas and ripe pineapple are so sweet they can be used as a sweetener.

OPTIONAL AND DELICIOUS INGREDIENTS FOR COOKIES AND OTHER SWEETS

Cashew meal, almond or pecan meal

Pumpkin seed meal or chopped seeds

Lemon peel

Orange peel

Any diced, dried fruit

Grated apples

Date pieces

Dehydrated orange, lemon, lime peel (ground)

Other combinations that can be eaten immediately as dessert, salad or semi-sweet fruit sauces, or frozen for popsicles, sherbet or, with a little safflower oil or thick cream, made into ice cream:

Mashed bananas with finely crushed cranberries (a bit of honey can be added)

Bananas and blueberries

Bananas and grated apples

Bananas and pineapple

Bananas and finely chopped orange or tangerine

Bananas and coconut milk and/or meal

Bananas and whole or sprouted sunflower seeds

DRINKS and LIQUID MEALS

WATERMELON DINNER OR DIET

1 small to medium
  watermelon

Wash watermelon with pure soap, rinse thoroughly. Remove the rind. Juice. Remove the seeds and with some of the red meat, blend until like thin cream. Strain out the seed hull pulp with fine screen wire colander. Serve rind juice, then the seed "milk" and last, eat the pulp. Serves 3 or 4 for a complete, satisfying and cleansing meal.

Note: A watermelon diet of two to three weeks makes a marvelous health-restoring regimen. Water retention disappears in a day or two. If the dieter is overweight, he or she will lose pounds. The first or second day when toxins (poisons) in the body are being stirred up and flushed out there may be feelings of general malaise, fatigue and even a touch of nausea and headache. Another day or two and the dieter begins to feel good. Then the third or fourth day he or she feels great, with bounding energy, a clear-thinking mind and a general feeling of well-being. Every watermelon season we go on a two or three week diet. After the first few days, we anticipate every watermelon meal.

CANTALOUPE DINNER OR DIET

1 cantaloupe

Peel cantaloupe as thinly as possible. Seeds should be whirled in the blender and strained. Remember to sip seed "milk" and rind juice slowly, mixing as much saliva as possible with the drink before swallowing. This meal should be eaten immediately after preparation.

Note: The minerals are mainly in and very near the rind of fruits and vegetables. Honeydew, casaba and crenshaw can be treated exactly the same as watermelon. Cantaloupe and muskmelon can be, too, if scrubbed with a brush and rinsed thoroughly.

Note: Any fresh fruit or vegetable makes a great drink for minerals and vitamins. Using, for instance, a Chop-rite juicer, a combination of any vegetables and weeds, and mainly green leaves, makes a superb drink that can serve as a meal or as an appetizer-beverage before a vegetable.

TYPICAL GREEN DRINKS:

NO. 1 FALL FARE

Comfrey
Celery
Beet top
Violet Leaves

Turnip Top and/or Root
Buckwheat Lettuce
Zucchini
Jerusalem Artichoke

NO. 2 WINTER BRACER

Celery Leaves and Stalks
Carrot
Romaine or Lettuce
Cabbage

Alfalfa
Winter Squash
Potato

NO. 3 SPRING TONIC

Dandelion Leaves and Root
Lambsquarter
Asparagus
Celery

Mung Bean Sprouts
Radish and Tops
Rhubarb
Comfrey

NO. 4 SUMMER REFRESHER

Nasturtiums
Parsley
Leaf Lettuce
Swiss Chard
Green Peas
Green Beans

Tomato
(Peppermint, spearmint, Chinese parsley, onion or garlic may be added for extra flavor.)

NO. 5 AUTUMN APPETIZER

Cabbage
Pumpkin
Tomato
Okra

Crookneck Squash
Corn
Parsley

ALMOND MILK

½ cup almonds, chopped
1¾ cups water

Blend ½ cup water with nuts for 1 minute. Add remaining liquid, blend, then strain out pulp, if desired. Makes 2¼ cups.

Note: All nuts and edible seeds make nutritious milks. After making a few recipes anyone can create interesting, delicious drinks.

SESAME SEED MILK

½ cup sesame seeds (it
   blends easier if soaked a
   few hours)

2 cups water

½ teaspoon honey
   (optional)

Blend sesame and 1 cup water.
Add the honey and remaining
water, blend a few seconds and
strain if desired. Makes 2¼
cups.

Note: If you have no blender, use seed or nut meal and mix with an
eggbeater or shake in a tightly capped jar.

Note: Since sesame is a little strong in taste, other flavors may be
added. Some prefer to make a drink of half sesame and half sunflower or pumpkin seed. Decorticated sesame (white, dehulled)
may be used for a milder, more milk-like drink. However, the
unhulled is more nutritious.

VARIATION:
SUNFLOWER SEED BUTTERMILK

Make the same as sesame seed milk but use fermec instead of
water. If more sour flavor is desired, leave in a warm place for
several hours.

WHEAT MILK

1 cup 24-hour sprouted
   wheat

1½ cups water

2 dates or 1 teaspoon
   honey, ½ teaspoon fructose or 1 teaspoon pure
   maple syrup (optional)

Mix sprouted wheat with
sweetener and 1 cup water (or
soak water which give the
milk a bit stronger flavor) and
blend until creamy. Add the
remaining ½ cup, strain and
serve or refrigerate. Makes 2
cups.

CAROB "CHOCOLATE" MILK

1 glass seed, nut or grain
    milk
½ cup carob
    Vanilla, drop or two
1 teaspoon honey
    Pinch salt

To the glass of seed, nut or
grain milk, add the carob,
vanilla, honey and salt. Blend,
stir or shake in a sealed jar.

SMOOTHIES

(Made in your blender — Each serves one)

No. 1
1 banana
1 orange
¼ avocado
¼ cup water

No. 2
1 apple, chopped
1 cup pineapple
½ cup fermec or heavy soy
    milk

No. 3
1 banana
½ cup raw carob powder
½ cup sprouted wheat milk

No. 4
1 cup blackberries, blue-
    berries, raspberries or
    strawberries
1 banana
¼ cup fermec, soy milk or
    fruit juice (berry seeds
    may be strained out if
    pureed first, before
    adding banana)

No. 5
1 apple, chopped
6 prunes, soaked
½ cup apple and/or prune
    juice

No. 6
6 dates
1 cup pineapple
¼ cup coconut
½ cup coconut milk or
    fermec

No. 7
1 cup raisin grapes
1 apple, chopped
¼ avocado
¼ cup apple juice or water

BREAKFAST CEREALS
(For 1 or 2 Persons)

COCO DATENA

½ cup of sprouted wheat (or the wheat left after the fermec has been poured off)

¼ cup chopped, fresh coconut

3 or 4 dates, seeded and cut up

½ cup coconut milk or water

Blend. Top with more cut up dates or sliced banana. Serves 2.

BARLEY BREAKFAST

½ cup sprouted barley

½ cup soaked prunes

½ cup prune soak water

1 teaspoon oil (optional)

Blend. Top with prunes. Serves 1 or 2.

RICE-RAISIN CEREAL

½ cup sprouted sweet rice

½ cup soaked raisins

½ cup raisin soak water

1 teaspoon oil (optional)

Blend. Top with a few raisins. Serves 1 or 2.

RYE BRAN CEREAL

½ cup sprouted rye
½ cup soaked figs
½ cup fig soak water
 1 teaspoon oil (optional)

Blend rye, soak water, oil and one-half the figs until a textured cream. Serve immediately with the remaining figs on top. Serves 1 or 2.
Note: A good sweetener for this full-flavored cereal is 1 or 2 teaspoons of blackstrap molasses.

NEW FASHIONED OATMEAL

1 cup sprouted oats
¾ cup soak water from dried pear or pineapple
1 teaspoon oil (optional)
1 cup soaked pear or pineapple

Blend well the oats, soak water, oil and half the fruit. Serve with the remaining fruit on top. Serves 2 to 4.

BUCKWHEAT-APRICOT CEREAL

1 cup sprouted buckwheat
¾ cup buckwheat soak water
1 cup soaked apricots
½ cup water from apricots
1 tablespoon honey (optional)
1 teaspoon oil (optional)

Blend the buckwheat, soak water, honey and half the apricots until a textured cream. Top with the remaining apricots and serve. Serves 2 to 4.

CREAM OF BUCKWHEAT

1 cup sprouted buckwheat

½ cup buckwheat soak
  water

½ cup water

1 teaspoon oil (optional)

1 tablespoon carob flour
  (or soy flour)

1 to 3 teaspoons honey

1 pinch salt

Cream all together in blender and serve topped with frozen or fresh fruit as strawberries, peaches or blueberries. Serves 2 to 4.

GRANOLA

2 cups sprouted wheat

2 cups sprouted oats

2 cups sprouted buckwheat

2 cups sprouted soy pulp

2 cups raisins

1 cup nuts, chopped

1 cup dry dates, chopped

½ cup honey (optional)

Fine grind or grind twice. Dehydrate all the sprouted grains. Mix. Warm honey and dribble over warm, dehydrated grains. Mix in raisins and dates. Makes approximately 6 cups of granola.

Note: Some like to put dehydrated grains through seed mill before adding honey, fruit and nuts.

Appendix

VITAMIN AND MINERAL DATA

The vitamins and minerals, their functions, deficiency symptoms and natural sources listed below, are included for reference. It is not our role to advocate supplementing one's diet with them. There is such a great overlap in the causes of deficiencies that only a nutritionally, biochemically-oriented physician or therapist should be consulted to diagnose the problems and prescribe the diet and/or supplements.

Our purpose in compiling the following data is purely educational and informative. We wish, in so doing, to make clear to you, our readers, that foods as they occur in nature—fresh, unfired and unprocessed—contain all nutrients essential for a healthy body. With this in mind, one can use the lists as a guide in planning a diet regimen to fit his or her individual needs.

VITAMIN A

Functions: Essential to membrane tissue and resistance to infections in sinuses, lungs, air passages, gastro-intestinal tract, vagina and eyes; prevents night blindness, sensitivity to light; promotes growth, vitality, appetite and digestion; helps prevent aging and senility; helps counteract damaging effects of air pollution.

Signs of Deficiency: Cystitis, sinusitis, bronchitis, gastritis; loss of appetite, retarded growth, eye problems—night blindness, red eyes, bad vision; defective teeth; dry, scaly skin, psoriasis, acne, wrinkles, pimples.

Sources: Dark green leafy vegetables, orange and yellow fruits and vegetables such as carrots, yams, cantaloupes, apricots; whole grains, especially wheat, rice and oats, seeds and nuts; sprouts.

VITAMIN B COMPLEX

In all cooked foods, this brain and nerve-nourishing vitamin complex is partially or completely destroyed, depending on the intensity of heat and time of cooking.

Functions: Promotes digestion, growth and appetite; maintains health of nerves and brain; necessary for the quality and quantity of milk during lactation; increases pancreatic secretions, one of which is insulin; maintains adrenal, thyroid, anterior pituitary glands; improves heart and circulation; aids in production of hydrochloric adic; aids in protein-carbohydrate-fat metabolism; helps prevent tooth decay, edema, epileptic seizures, and a host of other degenerative diseases such as arthritis and Parkinson's diseases.

Signs of Deficiency: Eye problems (i.e. cataracts); ulcers, loss of appetite, poor digestion, skin eruptions, mental depression, edema, anemia, halitosis, colitis, premature aging and senility, sore mouth and eyes; loss of vigor and weight, constipation, subnormal temperature, pathological disorders of adrenals, thymus, ovaries, spleen, heart, testes, liver, thyroid, kidneys, brain and pituitary; tendency to diabetes, disorders of thyroid, nerves and blood.

Sources: Whole cereal grains, especially sprouted, and sprouted seeds and legumes, served raw, dark green leafy vegetables, raw fruits, brewer's yeast.

VITAMIN C
(Ascorbic Acid and the Bioflavonoids - C complex)

Functions: Essential for good collagen, the "glue" that holds the cells together; necessary for vital functions of all organs and glands, especially adrenals, thymus and thyroid; protects against all stress (physical and mental), toxic chemicals in food, air and water, drugs and such poisons as rattlesnake bite and bee sting; acts as natural antibiotic and general protector against toxic metals, as cadmium, lead, mercury; essential for oxygen metabolism and for healthy teeth and gums; promotes leucocytic and phagocytic activity.

Signs of Deficiency: Soft, bleeding gums, decaying teeth, spontaneous bruising and purpura, lowered resistance to all infections and the toxicity of drugs and airborne poisons; skin hemorrhages, nose bleed, anemia, toxic thyroid, premature aging, physical weakness, rapid breathing and heart beat; reduced adrenal secretions; tendency to ulcers, stomach and duodenal. Absence of Vitamin C causes scurvy.

Sources: All raw fruits and vegetables, especially red bell peppers, tomatoes, rose hips, citrus fruits, acerola cherries, green leafy vegetables and sprouts.

VITAMIN D

Functions: Essential for the utilization of calcium and other metals by the digestive tract; necessary for proper function of thyroid and parathyroid glands; assures proper formation of bones and teeth in children.

Signs of Deficiency: Rickets, tooth decay, pyorrhea, osteomalacia, osteoporosis, retarded growth, muscular weakness, low energy, lack of mineral assimilation and premature aging.

Sources: Exposure of uncovered skin to the sun whose rays change the ergosterol in the skin into Vitamin D; fish liver oils, raw milk, egg yolk, sprouted seeds, wheat grass juice, mushrooms.

VITAMIN E

Functions: Provides oxygen to tissues and cells; improves circulation; prevents and reduces scar tissue from burns, surgery and sores; retards aging; lessens menopausal disorders; essential for the health of reproductive organs; serves as an anti-coagulant; prevents death from blood clot; aids circulation; shields lungs and other respiratory organs from air pollution; necessary for treatment and prevention of arthritis, heart disease, burns, asthma, phlebitis, emphysema, varicose veins, leg ulcers, bed sores and a host of other problems; prevents calcium deposits on blood vessel walls; loss of motility of eye lens; aids in lessening arterial hypertension.

Signs of Deficiency: Degeneration of coronary system, heart disease, strokes, pulmonary embolism, sterility, pains in muscles, nerve system; eye and cerebral hemorrhage; dermatitis, eczema; fragility of red blood cells.

Sources: All raw and sprouted seeds and cereal grains, legumes, seeds, especially flax and nuts; wheat germ if it is no more than 3 or 4 days old (older, rancid germ contains no Vitamin E); eggs, dark green leafy vegetables.

VITAMIN F

Fuctions: Helps to prevent heart disease by lowering blood cholesterol; necessary for function of adrenal and other glands; promotes growth, healthy skin and mucous membranes. Helps in making calcium and phosphorus available to cells, and in protecting from radiation.

Signs of Deficiency: Skin problems as eczema, dry skin, acne, fatigue, retarded growth, prostate and menstrual disorders; falling hair, gallstones, constipation, friability of bones (especially in the elderly).

Sources: Unrefined, unprocessed vegetable oils such as flaxseed oil, sunflower oil, soy oil, safflower oil and corn oil. Avocado is also a good source of oil.

VITAMIN G

Functions: Growth and development factor; essential to proper calcium utilization and formation of erythrocytes.

Signs of Deficiency: Calcium deposits as cataracts of the eye; underdevelopment, anemia, pellagra.

Sources: Brewer's yeast, eggs, cereal germ.

VITAMIN K

Functions: Vital for blood clotting and liver function. Called the anti-hemorrhaging vitamin, it also aids in vitality and longevity.

Signs of Deficiency: Hemorrhaging anywhere in the body; premature aging and low energy.

Sources: Seeds, sprouts, raw milk, egg yolks, alfalfa, kelp. Friendly bacteria in healthy intestines will synthesize Vitamin K.

VITAMIN T

Functions: Helps in correction of nutritional anemia and hemophilia and in forming blood platelets; helps improve failing memory.

Sources: Sesame seeds, raw and sprouted; sesame seed butter, some seed oils and raw egg yolk.

MINERALS

CALCIUM (Ca)

Functions: Vital for all muscle and activity of the body; needed for building and maintenance of bones, for normal growth, heart action, blood clotting; essential for normal pregnancy and lactation, for phosphorus, Vitamins A, C and D utilization; must be present for magnesium to be utilized. There needs to be a balance between calcium and magnesium for both to be used normally by the body.
Signs of Deficiency: Fragile, porous bones, heart problems; insomnia, tooth decay, nervousness and irritability, poor growth, muscle spasms, cramps, and rickets.
Sources: Sesame seeds (more than in milk), egg yolk, milk and milk products, dark green leafy vegetables such as dandelion, Romaine, spinach, kale, broccoli and brussel sprouts; kelp and sea plants.

CHLORINE (Cl)

Functions: Aids liver in detoxifying the body; necessary for the production of hydrochloric acid which is used in the stomach for digestion of proteins.
Signs of Deficiency: Disturbance of levels of fluids in the body; indigestion and poor assimilation of foods.
Sources: Kelp, dulse and other sea plants, dark green leafy vegetables, avocado, oats, asparagus, tomatoes, sea fish.

CHROMIUM (Cr)

Functions: Necessary for utilization of sugars; involved with activity of hormones and enzymes; aids in metabolism of cholesterol; identified as glucose tolerance factor; helps regulate serum cholesterol.

Signs of Deficiency: Diabetes, hypoglycemia (low blood sugar) and/or hyperglycemia (high blood sugar), heart disease, hardening of the arteries, high serum cholesterol.
Sources: Whole cereal grains (preferably sprouted), brewer's yeast, raw sugar cane, mushrooms and liver.

COBALT (Co)

Functions: Combines in hemoglobin-type molecule to synthesize Vitamin B_{12}; essential for formation of hemoglobin.
Signs of Deficiency: Pernicious anemia.
Sources: Comfrey, alfalfa, liver, some green leafy vegetables.

COPPER (Cu)

Functions: Essential for the absorption of iron; helps in development of nerves, bones, connective tissues and brain; aids protein metabolism, maintaining hair color; essential for RNA production.
Signs of Deficiency: Anemia, heart and digestive problems, graying of hair, respiration difficulty, hair loss.
Sources: Found in such iron-rich foods as legumes (peas, beans, etc.) leafy green vegetables, whole grains and their sprouts, almonds, raisins, prunes, liver.

FLUORINE (F)

Functions: Useful against infections; necessary in formation of healthy bones and teeth; too much, as in fluoridated water, is toxic and causes brown spots on teeth.
Signs of Deficiency: Weakened tooth enamel and calcium deficient bones.
Sources: Whole grain oats, seeds, carrots, green vegetables, almonds, milk, vegetable tops (especially beets).

IODINE (I)

Functions: Essential for the health and function of the thyroid gland which regulates much of the body's activity, both mental and physical; regulates energy, body weight and metabolism; helps maintain healthy skin.

Signs of Deficiency: Enlargement of thyroid gland and goiter; fatigue, loss of sexual interest, anemia, overweight, altered pulse rate, low blood pressure, heart disease and high cholesterol.
Sources: Dulse, kelp and other sea plants; green leafy vegetables and green tops of root vegetables (i.e. turnips and beets), pineapple, citrus fruits, watercress, sea foods, fish liver oils and egg yolks.

IRON (Fe)

Functions: Necessary for formation of red blood cells (hemoglobin) which transport oxygen to each and every body cell. Good quality hemoglobin provides resistance to disease and stress.
Signs of Deficiency: Anemia, weakness, headaches, pale skin, shortness of breath, difficulty in concentating, lack of interest and vigor, apathy towards sex.
Sources: Brewer's yeast, blackstrap molasses, raisins, prunes, nuts, seeds, whole grains, sea plants, sprouts, liver, egg yolks, alfalfa, green leafy vegetables and legumes.

LITHIUM (Li)

Functions: Involved with the involuntary nervous system; aids in metabolism of sodium and its transferance to muscles and nerves.
Signs of Deficiency: Mental and nerve problems, especially paranoia and/or schizophrenia.
Sources: Sea water, kelp; some mineral waters.

MAGNESIUM (Mg)

Functions: Essential for enzyme activity; aids in body's use of the B vitamins and Vitamin E, fats and other minerals, especially calcium; helps provide good bones and muscle tone; contributes to a healthy heart; balances acid-alkaline condition of the body; helps prevent build-up of cholesterol; necessary for normal, healthy heart function.
Signs of Deficiency: Muscle cramps, kidney stones and damage, heart attacks, atherosclerosis, disorientation and nervousness, epilepsia and faulty protein utilization. A prolonged deficiency causes the body to lose calcium and potassium, creating a deficiency in those and other metals; involved in protein synthesis.
Sources: Sesame, sunflower, pumpkin seeds, nuts (especially

almonds), whole grains, green leafy vegetables (i.e. kale, celery, dandelion, chard and endive), alfalfa, soybean (particularly sprouted), apples, peaches and lemons.

MANGANESE (Mn)

Functions: Vital to enzymes involved with the utilization of proteins, carbohydrates and fats; aids in reproduction; involved with nourishment and coordination responses between brain, muscles and nerves; with the help of choline, aids in digestion and absorption of fats.

Signs of Deficiency: Digestive problems, asthma, poor balance, sterility, bone deformity and abnormal growth.

Sources: All dark green leafy vegetables, apricots, oranges, blueberries, the outer coat of grains (bran) and nuts, legumes, raw egg yolk, kelp and sea plants.

MOLYBDENUM (Mo)

Functions: Helps prevent copper poisoning (cases of copper poisoning have greatly increased since copper tubing for bathrooms and kitchens began replacing conventional iron pipes); works together with some enzymes in the oxidation process; necessary for carbohydrate metabolism.

Signs of Deficiency: "Where molybdenum is lacking in the soil, the land is barren," says Dr. Carl C. Pfeiffer in *Mental and Elemental Nutrients.* Deficiencies have not as yet been positively identified. However, all tissues need a trace of molybdenum. From what is known to date, it seems entirely possible that sexual impotency, dental caries and cancer of the esophagus may be signs of molybdenum deficiency.

Sources: (In order of percentage found in foods.)
Whole buckwheat, lima beans, fresh wheat germ, soybeans, barley, lentils, oats, sunflower seeds, whole grain rye and eggs.

PHOSPHORUS (P)

Functions: Works in conjunction with calcium, in correct balance, for formation and maintenance of teeth and bones; essential for normal mental and nerve activities; major involvement with acid-alkaline balance of tissues and blood, and also carbohydrate metabolism.

Signs of Deficiency: Weakness, reduced sexual desire, retarded growth, poor bone mineralization, lowered brain and nerve performance.

Sources: Nuts, seeds, whole grains, legumes, sprouts, dairy products, dried fruits, egg yolks, and fish.

POTASSIUM (K)

Functions: Prevents overacidity by acting as agent to keep acid-alkaline balance in tissues and blood; necessary for muscle contraction; since the heart is a muscle, potassium is essential to proper heart function, especially the heart beat; necessary for normal nervous system; stimulates endocrine and other hormone production; aids kidneys to detoxify blood. There must be a proper balance between potassium and sodium (salt) for both to function normally.

Signs of Deficiency: Edema, sodium poisoning, high blood pressure and heart disease and/or failure; low blood sugar (hypoglycemia), weakness, exhaustion, mental and nervous problems and constipation.

Sources: Vegetables (particularly dark green leafy ones), nuts, seeds (sunflower and pumpkin), oranges, bananas and potatoes with peelings.

SELENIUM (Se)

Functions: Has role similar to Vitamin E as anti-oxidant; helps conserve the body's use of that vitamin; protects hemoglobin in red blood cells from oxidation damage; protects against mercury poisoning; helps to prohibit cancer cell proliferation; slows the aging process.

Signs of Deficiency: Premature aging, liver malfunction, muscle atrophy.

Sources: Brewer's yeast, kelp, sea plants, whole cereal grains, organically grown vegetables and fruits and sprouts.

SILICON (Si)

Functions: Necessary for strong bones, teeth and nails and good hair growth; aids in protecting and healing body against skin problems and irritations in membranes.

Signs of Deficiency: Thinning hair, wrinkles, brittle fingernails, osteoporosis, insomnia.

Sources: Sprouts (especially alfalfa), kelp, young green plants, strawberries, grapes, beets, almonds, sunflower seeds, steelcut oats (fresh).

SODIUM (Na)

Functions: Sodium, potassium and chlorine maintain osmatic pressure necessary for the absorption of nutrients from intestines into the blood; they maintain body fluids at normal levels; they change into electrically charged ions which transport nerve impulses; sodium must be present for hydrochloric acid production in the stomach; necessary for other glandular secretions.

Signs of Deficiency: Although sodium deficiencies are infrequent, they can result from prolonged ingestion of diuretics, excessive perspiration or chronic diarrhea which may cause weakness, heat prostration, nausea, apathy, breathing problems.

Sources: Sea water, kelp, sea salt, celery, sea plants, Romaine lettuce, asparagus.

SULFUR (S)

Functions: Essential for beautiful hair, nails and skin, hence called the "beauty mineral". Helps in conserving oxygen in the cells.

Signs of Deficiency: Eczema, blemishes, rashes of the skin; brittle nails and hair, problems in joints.

Sources: Watercress, horseradish, radish, celery, onion, turnip, nasturtium, fish, soybeans.

ZINC (Zn)

Functions: Vital for synthesis of DNA and RNA and body protein; along with insulin, aids in carbohydrate and energy metabolism; helps the healing of wounds and burns; aids in ridding the body of carbon dioxide; vital in normal growth and tissue respiration, and especially reproductive organs.

Signs of Deficiency: Underdeveloped sexual organs, enlargement

of prostate gland, birth defects, retarded growth, subnormal sex activity, low resistance to infections, sterility, slow healing of skin diseases, cuts and burns, hair loss, apathy, dandruff.
Sources: Sprouted and fermented seeds and grains as in the seed cheeses and Essene breads. Zinc in seeds and grains, "locked" in by phytin, is "unlocked" in sprouting and/or fermenting. Also found in natural seeds (especially pumpkin), brewer's yeast, raw milk, eggs, oysters (highest known source), green leafy vegetables, herring and nuts.

Botanical Families Of Edible Plants

Apple Family
Apple
Pear
Quince

Plum Family
Plum
Prune
Cherry
Peach
Apricot
Nectarine
Almond

Laurel Family
Avocado
Cinnamon
Bay leaves

Olive Family
Green olive
Ripe olive

Heath Family
Cranberry
Blueberry

Gooseberry Family
Gooseberry
Currant

Honeysuckle Family
Elderberry

Citrus Family
Orange
Grapefruit
Lemon
Lime
Tangerine
Kumquat

Ananas Family
Pineapple

Papal Family
Papaya

Grape Family
Grape
Raisin
Cream of tartar

Myrtle Family
Allspice
Cloves
Pimento
Paprika
Guava

Mint Family
Mint
Peppermint
Spearmint
Thyme
Sage
Marjoram

Mint Family (continued)
Savory

Pepper Family
Black pepper

Nutmeg Family
Nutmeg

Ginger Family
Ginger
Tumeric
Cardamon

Pine Family
Juniper
Pinon Nut

Orchid Family
Vanilla

Madder Family
Coffee

Tea Family
Tea

Pedalium Family
Sesame (Seed)

Mallow Family
Okra (Gumbo)
Cotton(seed)

Stercula Family
Cocoa

Birch Family
Filbert
Hazelnut

Mulberry Family
Mulberry
Fig
Hop
Breadfruit

Maple Family
Maple Syrup

Palm Family
Coconut
Date
Sage

Lecythis Family
Brazil Nut

Poppy Family
Poppy Seed

Walnut Family
English Walnut
Black Walnut
Butternut
Hickory Nut
Pecan

Cashew Family
Cashew
Pistachio
Mango

Beech Family
Chestnut

Fungi
Mushroom
Yeast

Miscellaneous
Honey
Papaya
Mango

Grains
Wheat
Rye
Barley
Corn
Oats
Rice
Wild Rice
Sorghum
Cane

Spurge Family
Tapioca

Arrowroot Family
Arrowroot

Linum Family
Flaxseed

Arum Family
Taro

Buckwheat Family
Buckwheat
Rhubarb

Potato Family
Potato
Tomato
Eggplant
Red Pepper
Green Pepper
Chili

Composite Family
Leaf Lettuce
Head Lettuce
Endive
Escarole

**Composite Family
(continued)**
Artichoke
Dandelion
Oyster Plant
Chicory

Legumes
Navy Bean
Kidney Bean
Lima Bean
String Bean
Mung
Soy Bean
Lentil
Black-eyed Pea
Pea
Peanut
Licorice
Acacia
Senna

Mustard Family
Mustard
Cabbage
Cauliflower
Broccoli
Brussel Sprouts
Turnip
Rutabaga
Kale
Collard
Kohlrabi
Radish
Horseradish
Watercress

Gourd Family
Pumpkin
Squash
Cucumber
Cantaloupe

**Gourd Family
(continued)**
Muskmelon
Honeydew
Persian Melon
Casaba
Watermelon

Lily Family
Asparagus
Onion
Garlic
Leek
Chive
Aloes

Goosefoot Family
Beet
Spinach
Swiss Chard

Parsley Family
Parsley
Parsnip
Carrot
Celery
Celeriac
Caraway
Anise
Dill
Coriander
Fennel

**Morning Glory
Family**
Sweet Potato
Yam

Sunflower Family
Jerusalem Artichoke
Sunflower Seed

**Pomegranate
Family**
Pomegranate

Ebony Family
Persimmon

Rose Family
Raspberry
Blackberry
Loganberry
Youngberry
Dewberry
Strawberry
Nectarberry

Banana Family
Banana

Miscellaneous
Jicama
Nopal
Carob

TABLE OF FOOD COMPOSITION

FRUITS	Measure	Weight g	Calories	Protein g	Fats g	Carbohydrates g	Calcium mg	Iron mg	Magnesium mg
Apples, raw, whole	1 med	130	76	0.3	0.8	17.0	9.0	0.39	10.4
Apricots, raw	1 med	38	19	0.4	0.1	4.1	6.5	0.19	4.6
Avocado	1 lg	216	361	4.5	33.0	12.0	22.0	1.30	97.0
Banana, raw	1 med	150	128	1.6	0.3	30.0	12.0	1.10	49.5
Blackberries, raw	1 cup	144	84	1.7	1.3	17.0	46.0	1.30	45.0
Blueberries, raw	1 cup	140	87	1.0	0.7	19.0	21.0	1.40	8.4
Cantaloupe, raw	¼	100	30	0.7	0.1	7.5	14.0	0.40	16.0
Cherries, sour, raw	1 cup	200	116	2.4	0.6	28.6	44.0	0.80	28.0
Cherries, sweet, raw	1 cup	200	140	2.6	0.6	32.0	44.0	0.80	22.5
Cranberries, raw	1 cup	100	460	0.4	0.7	10.8	14.0	0.50	-
Dates, dried	1 med	10	27	0.2	t	6.3	5.9	0.30	5.8
Elderberries, raw	1 cup	457	329	11.9	2.3	75.0	174.0	7.30	-
Figs, dried	1 lg	21	58	0.9	0.3	13.0	26.0	0.63	14.9
Figs, raw	1 med	38	30	0.5	0.1	6.8	13.0	0.23	7.6
Gooseberries	1 cup	150	59	1.2	0.3	14.6	27.0	0.75	13.5
Grapefruit, raw, red flesh, 5″ diam.	1 med	260	108	1.3	0.3	25.0	46.0	1.14	31.2
Grapes, American Concord	1 cup	153	106	2.0	1.5	21.0	24.0	0.61	19.9
Grapes, European, Muscat, or Tokay	1 cup	160	107	1.0	0.5	25.0	19.0	0.64	9.6
Grapes, green, seedless	1 cup	200	102	1.0	0.2	27.2	16.0	0.60	-

Phosphorus mg	Potassium mg	Sodium mg	Vitamin A IU	(Thiamine) B_1 mg	(Riboflavin) B_2 mg	Vitamin B_6 mg	Vitamin B_{12} mcg	Folic Acid mg	Niacin mg	Vitamin C mg	Vitamin E mg
13.0	143	1.0	117	0.040	0.03	0.039	0	0.003	0.13	5.20	0.40
8.7	107	0.4	1,026	0.010	0.02	0.023	0	0.001	0.23	0.38	-
91.0	1,305	8.6	626	0.240	0.43	0.907	0	0.060	3.46	31.00	-
39.0	555	1.5	285	0.080	0.09	0.765	0	0.010	1.05	15.00	0.33
27.0	245	1.4	288	0.040	0.06	0.075	0	0.021	0.60	30.00	-
18.0	113	1.0	140	0.040	0.08	0.094	0	0.011	0.70	20.00	-
16.0	251	12.0	3,400	0.040	0.03	0.086	0	0.007	0.60	33.00	0.14
38.0	218	4.0	2,000	0.100	0.12	0.170	-	0.012	0.80	20.00	-
38.0	382	4.0	220	0.100	0.12	0.064	0	0.012	0.80	20.00	-
10.0	2	82.0	40	0.030	0.02	0.040	-	-	0.10	11.00	-
6.3	65	0.1	5	0.016	0.01	0.015	0	-	0.20	0	-
127.0	1,371	-	2,742	0.320	0.27	-	-	-	2.29	-	-
16.0	134	7.1	17	0.020	0.02	0.037	0	0.007	0.15	0	-
8.4	74	0.8	30	0.020	0.02	0.043	0	0.010	0.15	0.76	-
22.5	233	1.5	435	-	-	-	-	-	-	49.50	-
46.0	385	2.9	1,144	0.160	0.06	0.090	0	0.010	0.57	105.00	0.58
18.0	242	4.6	153	0.080	0.05	0.120	0	0.010	0.46	6.12	-
32.0	277	4.8	160	0.080	0.05	-	-	-	0.48	6.40	-
26.0	220	8.0	140	0.080	0.02	-	-	-	0.40	4.0	-

TABLE OF FOOD COMPOSITION

FRUITS	Measure	Weight g	Calories	Protein g	Fats g	Carbohydrates g	Calcium mg	Iron mg	Magnesium mg
Lemon juice, fresh	1 T	15	4	0.1	t	1.2	1.0	0.03	4.5
Nectarine, raw	1 med	87	50	0.5	t	12.0	3.1	0.39	11.3
Olive, green, pickled	1 lg	7	9	0.1	0.9	0.1	4.3	0.11	1.54
Olive, ripe, canned	1 lg	7	13	0.1	1.4	0.2	7.4	0.12	-
Orange, fresh	1 med	180	88	1.8	0.4	20.0	74.0	0.72	19.8
Papaya, raw	1 lg	400	156	2.4	0.4	40.0	80.0	1.20	-
Peach, fresh	1 med	114	43	0.7	0.1	10.0	10.0	0.57	11.4
Pears, fresh	1 med	182	111	1.3	0.7	27.8	15.0	0.60	12.7
Persimmon, Japanese, raw	1 med	125	96	0.9	0.5	22.0	7.5	0.38	10.0
Pineapple, raw	1 cup	140	73	0.5	0.3	17.0	24.0	0.70	17.0
Plum, fresh, 2″ Damson	1 med	60	29	0.3	t	6.7	7.2	0.30	5.4
Prunes, dried, raw	1 lg	10	26	0.2	0.1	6.2	5.1	0.39	0.4
Raisins, dried	1 cup	160	462	4.0	0.3	111.0	99.0	5.60	56.0
Raspberries, red, raw	1 cup	133	76	1.6	0.7	16.0	29.0	1.20	26.6
Strawberries, raw	1 cup	149	55	1.0	0.7	11.0	31.0	1.49	17.9
Tangerine, raw	1 lg	114	52	0.9	0.2	12.0	46.0	0.46	-
Watermelon, 4″ x 8″ piece	1 wedge	925	241	4.6	1.8	52.0	65.0	4.63	84.2

Phosphorus mg	Potassium mg	Sodium mg	Vitamin A IU	(Thiamine) B$_1$ mg	(Riboflavin) B$_2$ mg	Vitamin B$_6$ mg	Vitamin B$_{12}$ mcg	Folic Acid mg	Niacin mg	Vitamin C mg	Vitamin E mg
2.0	85	0.1	3	0.010	t	0.030	-	t	0.01	7.00	-
19.0	229	4.7	1,287	t	t	0.015	0	0.017	-	10.00	-
1.2	4	168.0	21	0	0	-	0	-	-	t	-
1.2	2	53.0	4.9	t	t	0.001	0	t	-	-	-
36.0	360	1.8	360	0.180	0.05	0.108	0	0.010	0.72	90.00	0.43
64.0	936	12.0	7,000	0.160	0.16	-	0	-	1.20	224.00	-
22.0	234	1.1	1,516	0.020	0.06	0.027	0	0.004	1.14	7.98	-
20.0	237	3.6	36	0.040	0.08	0.034	0	-	0.18	7.28	-
33.0	218	7.5	3,388	0.040	0.03	-	-	-	0.13	13.80	-
11.0	204	1.4	98	1.300	0.04	0.120	0	0.008	0.28	24.00	-
11.0	102	0.6	150	0.040	0.02	0.030	0	-	0.30	3.60	-
7.9	69	0.8	160	0.010	0.02	0.020	0	0.001	0.16	0.30	-
162.0	1,221	43.0	32	0.180	0.13	0.380	0	0.020	0.80	1.60	-
29.0	223	1.3	173	0.040	0.12	0.080	0	0.007	1.20	33.00	-
31.0	244	1.5	89	0.050	0.10	0.080	0	0.013	0.89	88.00	0.19
21.0	144	2.3	479	0.070	0.02	0.076	0	0.008	0.11	35.00	-
93.0	925	9.2	5,458	0.280	0.28	0.630	0	0.009	1.85	65.00	

TABLE OF FOOD COMPOSITION

NUTS, NUT PRODUCTS, AND SEEDS	Measure	Weight g	Calories	Protein g	Fats g	Carbohydrates g	Calcium mg	Iron mg	Magnesium mg
Almonds, dried	1 cup	140	765	26.0	76.0	26.0	328.0	6.58	378.0
Brazil nuts, unsalted	1 cup	300	1,962	42.0	201.0	32.7	558.0	10.00	675.0
Butternuts	5 avg	15	96	3.6	9.2	1.3	-	1.00	-
Cashews, unsalted	1 cup	100	569	15.0	45.0	26.0	39.0	3.80	274.0
Chestnuts, fresh	1 cup	200	382	5.8	3.0	84.2	54.0	3.40	82.0
Coconut, fresh	1 cup	100	346	3.5	35.3	9.4	13.0	1.70	46.0
Hazelnuts (filberts)	11 avg	15	97	1.6	9.5	3.0	38.0	0.50	27.6
Hickory nuts	15 sm	15	101	2.1	10.1	2.0	-	0.40	24.0
Peanuts, roasted, w/skin	1 cup	240	1,397	60.0	107.0	48.0	173.0	5.28	420.0
Pistachio nuts	1 cup	100	594	19.0	54.0	19.0	131.0	7.30	158.0
Pumpkin and Squash kernels	1 cup	230	1,271	67.0	107.0	35.0	117.0	26.00	-
Sesame seeds, dry, decorticated	1 cup	230	1,339	42.0	123.0	41.0	253.0	5.50	416.0
Sunflower seeds, dry	1 cup	100	560	24.0	43.0	19.0	120.0	7.10	38.0
Walnuts, Black	1 cup	100	628	21.0	59.6	15.1	t	6.00	190.0
Walnuts, English, raw	1 cup	100	651	15.0	59.0	15.0	99.0	3.10	131.0

Phosphorus mg	Potassium mg	Sodium mg	Vitamin A IU	(Thiamine) B_1 mg	(Riboflavin) B_2 mg	Vitamin B_6 mg	Vitamin B_{12} mcg	Folic Acid mg	Niacin mg	Vitamin C mg	Vitamin E mg
706.0	1,082	5.6	0	0.340	1.29	0.140	0	0.063	4.90	t	-
2,088.0	2,145	3.0	t	3.300	0.36	0.510	0	0.015	4.60	30.00	-
373.0	464	15.0	100	0.430	0.25	-	0	-	1.80	-	-
176.0	908	12.0	-	0.440	0.44	-	-	-	0.12	-	-
95.0	256	23.0	0	0.050	0.02	0.044	0	0.028	0.50	3.00	-
48.0	71	0.1	16	0.069	0.08	-	-	0.010	0.80	1.10	-
54.0	-	-	-	0.080	-	-	-	-	0	-	-
976.0	1,683	12.0	t	0.770	0.32	0.700	0	0.140	40.00	2.40	18.50
500.0	972	-	230	0.670	-	-	-	-	1.40	0	-
2,631.0	-	-	161	0.550	0.44	-	-	5.50	-	-	
1,361.0	-	-	-	0.410	0.30	-	-	-	12.40	0	-
837.0	920	30.0	50	1.960	0.23	-	-	-	5.40	-	-
570.0	460	3.0	300	0.220	0.11	-	-	0.077	0.70	-	-
380.0	450	2.0	30	0.330	0.13	0.730	0	0.080	0.90	2	

TABLE OF FOOD COMPOSITION

VEGETABLES	Measure	Weight g	Calories	Protein g	Fats g	Carbohydrates g	Calcium mg	Iron mg	Magnesium mg
Artichoke, raw	1 sm	100	44	2.9	0.2	10.6	51.0	1.30	-
Asparagus, raw	1 spear	16	4	0.4	t	0.8	3.5	1.60	-
Beans, green, cooked	1 cup	125	31	2.0	0.2	8.9	62.5	.75	40.0
Beans, Lima, green, raw	1 cup	160	197	13.0	0.8	35.4	83.2	4.50	10.7
Bean sproutes (mung beans) raw	1 cup	50	-	1.9	0.1	3.3	10.0	0.65	-
Cabbage, shredded, raw	1 cup	105	25	1.4	0.2	5.7	51.5	0.42	14.0
Cabbage, red, raw	1 cup	100	31	2.0	0.2	6.9	42.0	0.80	35.0
Carrots, sliced, raw	1 lg	100	42	1.1	0.2	9.7	37.0	0.70	23.0
Cauliflower, raw	1 cup	100	27	2.7	0.2	5.2	25.0	1.10	24.0
Celery, stalk, raw	1 lg	50	8	0.4	t	2.0	0.2	0.15	11.0
Chickpeas (garbanzos), dry, raw	½ cup	100	360	20.5	4.8	61.0	150.0	6.90	-
Chives, chopped, raw	1 T	10	3	0.2	t	0.6	7.0	0.20	-
Corn, on-the-cob, raw	1 ear	100	96	3.5	1.0	22.0	3.0	0.70	48.0
Cucumber, raw, not pared	½ med	50	8	0.5	t	1.7	13.0	0.60	6.0
Endive (escarole) raw	1 cup	228	46	3.9	0.2	9.3	17.8	39.00	22.8
Garlic	1 bulb	2	2	0.1	t	0.6	0.6	0.03	-
Kohlrabi, raw, sliced	1 cup	140	41	2.8	0.1	9.2	57.0	0.70	52.0
Leeks, raw	1 cup	200	104	4.4	0.6	22.4	104.0	2.20	46.0
Lettuce, Bibb, Boston	3½ oz	100	14	1.2	0.2	2.5	35.0	2.00	-
Lettuce, Iceberg (head)	3½ oz	100	13	0.9	0.1	2.9	20.0	0.50	11.0

Phosphorus mg	Potassium mg	Sodium mg	Vitamin A IU	(Thiamine) B_1 mg	(Riboflavin) B_2 mg	Vitamin B_6 mg	Vitamin B_{12} mcg	Folic Acid mg	Niacin mg	Vitamin C mg	Vitamin E mg
88.0	430	43.0	160	0.080	0.05	-	-	-	1.00	12.00	-
9.9	44	0.3	144	0.030	0.03	0.020	-	0.020	0.24	5.30	-
46.3	189	5.0	675	0.090	0.11	0.100	0	0.040	0.75	15.00	-
227.0	1,040	3.2	46.4	0.380	0.19	0.270	-	0.050	2.24	46.40	-
32.0	112	2.5	10	0.070	0.07	-	-	-	0.40	10.00	-
31.5	245	21.0	137	0.050	0.05	0.170	0	0.034	0.32	44.00	-
-	268	26.0	40	0.090	0.06	' -	-	-	0.40	61.00	-
36.0	341	47.0	11,000	0.060	0.05	0.150	0	0.008	0.60	8.00	0.11
56.0	295	13.0	60	0.110	0.11	0.210	0	0.022	0.70	78.00	-
14.0	171	63.0	120	0.020	0.02	0.030	0	0.004	0.15	4.50	0.19
331.0	797	26.0	50	0.310	0.15	0.54	-	0.130	2.00	-	-
4.0	25	-	580	0.080	0.13	-	-	-	0.10	6.00	-
111.0	280	-	400	.15	0.12	-	-	-	1.70	12.00	-
14.0	80	3.0	125	0.015	0.02	0.021	0	0.004	0.10	5.50	-
123.0	6,826	31.9	7,524	0.160	0.32	0.050	0	0.107	1.14	22.80	-
4.0	11	0.4	t	0.010	t	-	-	-	0.01	0.30	-
71.0	521	11.2	28	0.080	0.06	-	-	-	0.42	92.00	-
100.0	694	10.0	80	0.220	0.12	-	-	-	1.00	34.00	3.80
26.0	264	9.0	970	0.060	0.06	-	-	-	0.03	8.00	-
22.0	175	9.0	330	0.060	0.06	0.055	0	0.021	0.30	6.00	0.06

TABLE OF FOOD COMPOSITION

VEGETABLES	Measure	Weight g	Calories	Protein g	Fats g	Carbohydrates g	Calcium mg	Iron mg	Magnesium mg
Lettuce, leaf	3½ oz	100	18	1.3	0.3	3.5	68.0	1.40	-
Lettuce, Romaine	3½ oz	100	18	1.3	0.3	3.5	68.0	1.40	11.0
Onions, green, raw	1 bulb	8	4	0.1	t	0.8	3.2	0.05	-
Parsley, chopped, raw	1 cup	56	25	2.0	0.3	4.8	114.0	3.50	23.0
Peppers, sweet, green, raw	1 lg	100	22	1.2	0.2	4.8	9.0	0.70	18.0
Potato, baked, w/skin	1 med	100	93	2.6	0.1	21.1	9.0	0.70	22.0
Pumpkin, raw	½ cup	100	26	1.0	0.1	6.5	21.0	8.00	12.0
Radish, raw, red	1 sm	10	2	0.1	t	0.4	3.0	0.10	1.5
Rutabagas, raw	1 cup	150	69	1.6	1.5	16.5	99.0	0.60	22.5
Spinach, raw	1 cup	100	26	3.2	0.3	4.3	93	3.10	88.0
Squash, summer, raw	1 cup	200	38	2.2	0.2	8.4	56.0	0.80	32.0
Squash, winter, boiled, mashed	1 cup	200	76	2.2	0.6	18.4	40.0	1.00	34.0
Sweet potato, baked	1 sm	100	141	2.1	0.5	32.5	40.0	0.90	31.0
Tomato, raw	1 med	150	33	1.6	0.3	7.1	19.5	0.75	21.0
Turnip, raw	½ cup	100	30	1.0	0.2	6.6	39.0	0.50	20.0
Turnip, tops, raw	1 cup	100	28	3.0	0.3	5.0	246.0	1.80	58.0
Water chestnuts, Chinese, raw	4 avg	25	20	0.3	t	4.7	1.0	0.15	-
Watercress	1 cup	50	10	1.1	0.1	1.5	75.5	0.85	10.0

Phosphorus mg	Potassium mg	Sodium mg	Vitamin A IU	(Thiamine) B$_1$ mg	(Riboflavin) B$_2$ mg	Vitamin B$_6$ mg	Vitamin B$_{12}$ mcg	Folic Acid mg	Niacin mg	Vitamin C mg	Vitamin E mg
25.0	264	9.0	1,900	0.050	0.08	-	-	0.044	0.40	18.00	-
25.0	264	9.0	1,900	0.050	0.08	-	-	-	0.40	18.00	-
3.1	18	0.4	t	0.004	t	-	0	0.001	0.03	2.00	-
35.3	407	25.0	4,760	0.070	0.11	0.090	0	0.020	0.67	96.30	3.10
22.0	213	13.0	420	0.080	0.08	0.260	0	0.007	0.50	128.00	-
65.0	503	4.0	t	0.100	0.04	0.233	-	-	1.70	20.00	0.03
44.0	340	1.0	1,600	0.050	0.11	-	-	-	0.60	9.00	
3.1	32	1.8	1	0.003	t	t	0	0.001	0.03	2.60	-
58.5	360	7.5	870	0.110	0.11	-	-	-	1.60	64.30	-
51.0	470	71.0	8,100	0.100	0.20	-	-	-	0.60	51.00	-
58.0	404	2.0	820	0.100	0.18	0.126	-	0.034	2.00	44.00	-
64.0	516	2.0	7,000	0.080	0.20	0.182	0	0.024	0.80	16.00	-
58.0	300	12.0	8,100	0.090	0.07	0.218	0	0.015	0.70	22.00	-
40.5	366	1.5	1,390	0.090	0.06	0.150	0	0.012	1.95	34.50	0.60
30.0	268	49.0	-	0.040	0.07	-	-	-	0.60	36.00	
58.0	312	-	7,600	0.210	0.39	-	-	-	0.80	139.00	-
16.3	125	5.0	0	0.040	0.05	-	-	-	0.25	1.00	-
27.0	141	21.0	2,450	0.040	0.08	-	-	-	0.45	39.50	

Bibliography

ACCIARDO, MARCIA MADHURI. *Light Eating For Survival.* Wethersfield, CT: Omango D'Press, Publishers, 1977.

ADLER, KIEF. *Beyond The Staff Of Life.* Happy Camp, CA: Naturegraph Publishers, Inc., 1976.

AIROLA, PAAVO. *How To Get Well.* Phoenix, AZ: Health Plus, Publishers, P.O. Box 22001.

BRAGG, PAUL C. *The Miracle Of Fasting.* Santa Ana, CA: Health Science, 1974.

BUCKINGER, OTTO H. F. *About Fasting — A Royal Road To Healing.* Wellingborough, Northamptonshire: Thorsons Publishers Limited, 1976.

CARTER, ALBERT E. *The Miracles of Rebound Exercise.* Bothell, WA: The National Institute of Reboundology & Health, Inc., 1979.

CARTER, MILDRED. *Hand Reflexology: Key To Perfect Health.* West Nyack, NY: Parker Publishing Company, Inc., 1975.

DIAMOND, JOHN. *Your Body Doesn't Lie.* New York, NY: Warner Books, Inc., 1979.

FATHMAN, GEORGE and DORIS. *Live Foods.* Beaumont, CA: Ehret Literature Publishing Co., 1967.

FREDERICKS, CARLTON. *Psycho-Nutrition.* New York, NY: Grosset & Dunlap, A Filmways Company Publishers, 1978.

GERRAS, CHARLES, Editor. *Feasting On Raw Foods.* Emmaus, PA: Rodale Press, 1980.

HILLS, CHRISTOPHER. *Rejuvenating the Body.* Boulder Creek, CA: University of the Trees Press, 1979.

HUNSBERGER, EYDIEMAE and LEOFFLER, CRIS. *Eydiemae's Natural Recipes.* San Diego, CA: Production House Publishers, 1978.

KLINE, MONTE L. and STRUBE, W. P., JR. *Eat, Drink And Be Ready.* Fort Worth, TX: Harvest Press, Inc., 1977.

KULVINSKAS, VIKTORAS. *Sprouts For The Love Of Every Body.* Wethersfield, CT: Omango D'Press, 1978.

LAPPE, FRANCES MOORE. *Diet For A Small Planet.* New York, NY: Ballantine Books, 1975.

MUNROE, ESTHER. *Sprouts To Grow And Eat.* Brattleboro, VT: The Stephen Green Press, 1977.

PAULING, LINUS. *Vitamin C, The Common Cold, And The Flu.* San Francisco, CA: W. H. Freeman and Company, 1976.

PFEIFFER, CARL C. *Mental And Elemental Nutrients*. New Canaan, CT: Keats Publishing, Inc., 1975.

SHUTE, WILFRID. *Vitamin E Book*. New Canaan, CT: Keats Publishing, Inc., 1975.

WHYTE, KAREN CROSS. *The Complete Sprouting Cookbook*. San Francisco, CA: Troubador Press, 1973.

WIGMORE, ANN. *Be Your Own Doctor*. New York, NY: Hemisphere Press.

WILLIAMS, ROGER J. *Nutrition Against Disease*. New York, NY: Bantam Books, 1973.

WILLIAMS, ROGER J. and KALITA, DWIGHT K. *A Physician's Handbook On Orthomolecular Medicine*. New York, NY: Pergamon Press, 1977.

Index